ANARCHISM

A THEORETICAL ANALYSIS

For Eileen and Jon

ANARCHISM

A THEORETICAL ANALYSIS

ALAN RITTER

CAMBRIDGE UNIVERSITY PRESS

Cambridge

London   New York   New Rochelle

Melbourne   Sydney

Published by the Press Syndicate of the University of Cambridge
The Pitt Building, Trumpington Street, Cambridge CB2 1RP
32 East 57th Street, New York, NY 10022, USA
296 Beaconsfield Parade, Middle Park, Melbourne 3206, Australia

First published 1980

Printed in Great Britain by
Western Printing Services Ltd, Bristol

British Library Cataloguing in Publication Data
Ritter, Alan
Anarchism.
1. Anarchism and anarchists
I. Title
335'.83'01   HX833   80-40589
ISBN 0 521 23324 0

CONTENTS

Contents

ACKNOWLEDGMENTS

Preliminary versions of material in Chapters 5 and 6 appeared originally in 'Anarchism and Liberal Theory in the Nineteenth Century', *Bucknell Review*, 19 (Fall 1971); in 'Godwin, Proudhon and the Anarchist Justification of Punishment', *Political Theory*, vol. 3, no. 1 (February 1975), pp. 69–87 (Sage Publications, Inc.); and in 'The Anarchist Justification of Authority', *Anarchism: Nomos XIX*, edited by J. Roland Pennock and John W. Chapman (© 1978 by New York University, by permission of New York University Press). Portions of these articles are here reprinted by permission of their publishers.

A grant from the National Endowment for the Humanities helped me to get started on this book. Colleagues and students helped me to complete it. I would like particularly to thank Alfred Diamant, Milton Fisk, Norman Furniss, Richard Hiskes, Eileen Janzen, Jerome Mintz, Bernard Morris, Timothy Tilton and George Wright for their suggestions and support.

INTRODUCTION

The main purpose of this book is to establish the right of anarchists to a leading voice in the debate among political theorists over how a good society should be created, organized and run. That anarchists deserve such a voice would have seemed ludicrous as recently as ten years ago, when they were still generally regarded as muddled preachers of chaos or naive projectors of dreams. In the late sixties, however, commentators began to find the anarchists more intellectually respectable. Their arguments for a society free of law and government were then revealed as credible enough to render political theory service, if only as a challenge to its deeply ingrained habit of taking the need for government for granted.[1] This book carries forward the work of claiming a place in political theory for anarchists by showing that their arguments, besides being plausible enough to serve as a foil or corrective to uncritically statist views, are also inherently convincing. If the analysis that follows is acceptable, anarchists must be accorded no less a voice than partisans of theories such as democracy or socialism in debate concerning the nature of a good society.

Although anarchists are no longer excluded from political theory altogether, they have not received the place this book claims for them, partly because their thought is still believed to suffer from a seriously discrediting contradiction. Anarchists favor untrammelled freedom. Yet to control behavior in their good society they use the constraint of public censure, whose strictures interfere with the freedom they endorse. The conflict between their espousal of freedom and their resort to censure not only opens anarchists to being disparaged as inconsistent, it exposes them to the more onerous charge of supporting freedom as a pretence. The denigration of their support for freedom as masking a deep antipathy to it began in 1798, in a pamphlet attacking the first anarchist, William Godwin. The author of the pamphlet, William Proby, decried Godwin's commitment to freedom as deceptive on the ground that his good society, though it eschewed physical coercion, used the 'tyranny of public opinion' as a fetter. 'There is no tyranny more forcible, for the mind, wearied by repeated systematic attacks, at last becomes a convert, or quits the field in despair, feeling a slavery in its utmost recesses, the more degrading because exercised by chains emanating from its own substance.'[2] Proby's view of the anarchists as not just confused, but downright devious in their espousal of freedom, has never lacked defenders. Commentators are still busy unmasking anarchists as 'proselytising aristocrats' with a yen for 'puritanical constraint', determined to exercise 'enlightened tutelage' over the people, if not against them.[3] Unless the anarchists' praise of freedom and resort to censure are proved logically compatible, their claim to a full place in political theory must fail. For arguments which include contentions that are patently inconsistent disqualify as theory, even if they are not intended to deceive.

The view of anarchists as inconsistent for praising freedom while imposing censure rests on two premises: that freedom is their chief political value, and that it is curtailed severely by the censure they impose. This book argues for the consistency of the anarchists in praising freedom while imposing censure by refuting these premises. Freedom is exhibited in the following analysis as having subordinate worth for anarchists; their censure is shown to be a complex practice, whose effects on freedom are ambivalent. Once the censure of the anarchists is recognized as having ambivalent effects on a freedom that lacks supreme value in their eyes, their consistency in espousing it becomes obvious. Though their censure curtails freedom, they are warranted logically to espouse it, since it also supports freedom, and since they do not value freedom above all.

In establishing the right of anarchists to a leading voice in political theory, clearing them of inconsistency is a preliminary step. The main task is to show the power of their argument as social criticism and as a guide to action. This book takes a novel thesis about the goal of anarchism as the point of departure for accomplishing this task. Anarchists are portrayed in the following analysis as seeking to combine the greatest individual development with the greatest communal unity. Their goal is a society of strongly separate persons who are strongly bound together in a group. In a full-fledged anarchy, individual and communal tendencies, now often contradictory, become mutually reinforcing and coalesce. By serving the anarchists as a goal and inspiration, this ideal of communal individuality, as it will here be called, does much to control the structure of their argument. It helps define the targets of their social criticism; it gives their strategy limits and direction; and it guides their description of an anarchist social order. It is by tracing out the implications for their theory of their commitment to communal individuality that the following analysis exhibits the strength of the anarchists' thought. Once the leading role played in their theory by communal individuality is appreciated, their argument is revealed as having altogether unsuspected coherence, originality and political appeal.

Anarchists are not the only theorists who take individuality and community, seen as mutually dependent values, as their chief political objective. Noteworthy others who have done so are their contemporaries Hegel and Marx. Since the credentials of these thinkers are so much stronger than the anarchists', it is natural to presume that to learn how the search for communal individuality affects and enlivens political theory they and not the anarchists should be consulted. Yet, though Hegel and Marx are on most points the more penetrating thinkers, as theorists of communal individuality the anarchists can teach more.

In what Hegel calls a rational state, each subject achieves 'complete development' of 'personal individuality' and also 'recognizes the community as his substantial groundwork and end'. These aspects of a rational state are intimately connected for Hegel. There can be no intense community unless individuality reaches 'its culmination in the extreme of self-subsistent personal particularity', while individuality needs the context of community for its development. People who live 'as private persons

3

for their own ends alone' cannot be individuals. It is only as members of a community that they have 'objectivity, genuine individuality, and an ethical life'.[4] Marx has a quite different view from Hegel of the path to individuality and community, but he agrees that they are mutually reinforcing. Everyone at the final stage of socialism engages in productive activities 'which confirm and realize his individuality', while also being 'an expression of social life'. Community both 'produces man as man' and 'is produced by him', because individuality and community are reciprocally dependent.[5] Thus for Marx, as for Hegel and the anarchists, a nourishing interplay must draw individuality and community together, if they are to be complete.

Marx and Hegel, being in the first rank of political theorists, might be expected to explain more plausibly than the anarchists just how individuality and community, which tend to clash, can be made so mutually reinforcing that both are maximized. Yet what they say about this matter is so deficient that the anarchists' views are more convincing.

Hegel makes legal government the seedbed in which communal individuality grows. Now one point which will become clear in the course of this book, and which has much immediate credibility, is that legal government, being remote, punitive, and inflexible, is not very congenial to communal individuality. It is true that Hegel tries to purge his rational state of the attributes that normally encumber legal government, but this attempt is futile, since these attributes mark every state.[6] Marx, who ably criticizes Hegel for thinking that communal individuality can reach completion under the aegis of legal government, relies on it in his good society much less. Community and individuality, in communist society, are therefore better able to develop. Yet even Marx stops short of the anarchist exclusion of legal government from the stage when individuality and community, now fully reinforcing, completely merge. The elements of legal government which communist society retains prevent it from being as hospitable as anarchy to communal individuality's full growth.

Though the comparative paucity of legal government in Marx's good society, and its correlatively greater reliance on nonlegal institutions, give it an advantage over Hegel's as the setting in which communal individuality develops, this advantage is offset by the vagueness with which it is portrayed. Marx limits himself to sketchy hints about the structure of the good society, while Hegel gives a detailed description. Since it is anything but obvious how a society must be organized so that individuality and community culminate in a reinforcing merger, Marx, by failing to work out in concrete detail the conditions for this outcome, marred his theory with a disconcerting gap.

The anarchists' theory is free of the faults that blemish Marx's and Hegel's. By banning legal government entirely from their good society, they rid it altogether of the impediments which in the Hegelian state hamper communal individuality severely and which continue to interfere with it under Marx's communism. And by describing their good society concretely, they protect it from the indeterminacy which, for achieving communal individuality, is communism's special defect. Because the anarchists work out in detail, and with no resort to legal government, how to create, organize and maintain a regime in which communal individuality flourishes, it is they who have the most to teach about the value of this project for the debate in political theory over the nature of the best regime.

The arguments treated in this book as representing the gist of anarchism are drawn from the four authors – Godwin, Pierre-Joseph Proudhon, Michael Bakunin and Peter Kropotkin – whose contributions to anarchist theory are universally regarded as most seminal. These writers, who succeeded each other within the discretely bounded period between the French and Russian Revolutions, worked out a coherent set of original arguments, which, while continuing to be influential, have not developed much since Kropotkin's time. Hence, to comprehend anarchism as a political theory, the writings of more recent anarchists need not be considered. There is, however, one nineteenth-century writer besides the four founders who, because his arguments have affinities with theirs, and because of his influence on later anarchists, may be thought unfairly excluded from the following analysis. This writer is Max Stirner.

Some anarchists, most notably Kropotkin, have acknowledged Stirner as a forebear. But this acknowledgment does not mean that he must be included in this book, because it proves nothing about the standing of his argument as systematic thought. Stirner's argument is anarchist in its political conclusions. He rejects law and government at least as unconditionally as do the four anarchists being studied here, and his projected 'union of egoists' is in its statelessness as much an anarchist society as those envisaged by the founding four. But Stirner's argument differs from theirs in a way that debases it as a theory: its backing for these anarchist conclusions is anything but cogent. Stirner opposes government and supports an anarchist society on the moral basis of ethical egoism, a principle which enjoins each agent to strive for nothing but his selfish advantage or amusement, and hence for that of others only so far as it conduces to his own. The Stirnerian egoist cares not a jot whether others do what is in their interest: their service to his interest is his sole concern. 'No one is a person to be respected. . .but solely. . .an object in which I take an interest or else do not, an interesting or uninteresting object, a usable or unusable person.'[7] The state is denounced by Stirner for interfering with ethical egoism; the union of egoists, his anarchist society, is recommended for allowing it free reign. Yet both of these claims about the political implications of ethical egoism, which must be true if Stirner's defense of anarchism is to be cogent, are surely false. A state is admirably suited to a seeker of personal advantage, in situations where he controls it, for it is then a means for making others serve his ends. As for an anarchist society, since the voluntary cooperation on which it rests requires each to strive for others' advantage at least somewhat, it is hardly the arrangement that ethical egoists should create. Nor could they create it. For a stateless society of ethical egoists, each regarding the others as objects to be manipulated and exploited, would be impossibly discordant. Since Stirner's anarchism is probably undermined and is certainly not supported by the moral premise which is supposed to serve as its foundation, his argument lacks the cogency it needs to be included in this analytic study of anarchist thought.[8]

Introduction

The plan of this book is suggested by its overall approach. The first chapter tackles the problem of proving the anarchists consistent in their espousal of both liberty and censure. Chapter 2 argues for regarding communal individuality as their chief political objective. Having made the case for anarchists as seeking communal individuality, the book moves on, in Chapter 3, to trace out the implications of this objective for their somewhat varied yet basically similar models of the good society. Chapters 4 and 5 complete the project of analyzing the import for anarchists of their search for communal individuality by examining how it affects their social criticism and their strategy. The plausible, coherent anarchist theory, established as authentic in the first five chapters of the book, is subjected in the final chapters to comparison and evaluation. Chapter 6 compares anarchism with liberalism and socialism, the political positions with which it is most frequently identified, and finds that, despite its similarities to these close neighbors, it is nevertheless distinctive. In the seventh, concluding chapter, anarchism is judged as a political ideal and as a guide to action against standards of humane morality. No such evaluation can be conclusive. The point of this one is to acquit anarchists of unjust charges and to highlight the appealing features of their argument so as to vindicate it as more than intellectually respectable. If this chapter is successful, the criticisms which anarchists level against the modern state and their recommendations for how it should be replaced or altered will be revealed as worthy of more wholehearted endorsement than has generally been allowed.

Although the main purpose of this study is to vindicate anarchism as a theory, success in this purpose will spur readers to follow anarchism as a practice. Those who are convinced by the arguments in this book that anarchist theory is coherent, plausible and appealing need not of course join communes or found free schools, let alone attempt a revolution. But they cannot abstain entirely from anarchist endeavors without defending their inaction at least inwardly. To readers who find anarchist activity congenial, this book, if it succeeds, will be more welcome. For it will help them act by giving them theoretically grounded arguments to justify what might otherwise seem quixotic gestures. Anarchism, though studied here as theory, is a theory that asks constantly what to do. Hence the more fully it is accepted as theoretically convincing, the stronger will be its pressure as a goad.

1

LIBERTY AND PUBLIC CENSURE IN ANARCHIST THOUGHT

Anarchists are commonly regarded as extreme libertarians on the ground that they seek freedom above all else. It is natural to view them as libertarians in this sense, because their high esteem for freedom makes it more immediately plausible than any other value as their overriding aim. Godwin praises freedom as 'the most valuable of all human possessions'. Proudhon acclaims it as his 'banner and guide'. To Bakunin, who once described himself as 'a fanatic lover of liberty', it is 'the absolute source and condition of all good'. And Kropotkin seeks a form of society which 'will leave to the individual man complete and perfect freedom'.[1] It seems difficult to question the commitment to liberty of theorists who admire it as much as these.

Yet the reliance of anarchists on public censure to control behavior in their good society raises doubts whether their goal is liberty. In Godwin's anarchy 'the inspection of every man over the conduct of his neighbors...would constitute a censorship of the most irresistible nature', which 'no individual would be hardy enough to defy'; for 'there is no terror that comes home to the heart of vice like the terror of being exhibited to the public eye'. Proudhon depends on censure in a state of anarchy to 'act on the will like a force and make it choose the right course'. Bakunin follows Proudhon in regarding 'the collective and public spirit' of an anarchist society as 'the only great and all powerful authority...we can respect'. And Kropotkin is perfectly candid in explaining what to do 'when we see anti-social acts committed' in a state of anarchy. We must 'have the courage to say aloud in anyone's presence what we think of such acts'.[2] How can the anarchists be libertarians, determined to secure freedom above

9

Liberty and public censure

all else, when their social scheme relies so much on coercive public censure? Although interpreters of anarchism have long deemed this question crucial, no acceptable answer has yet been found.

Several types of argument are or can be advanced by anarchists to warrant viewing their search for liberty as compatible with their use of censure. This chapter finds, after examining these arguments, that only one of them is valid. But not even this one is strong enough to prove the anarchists consistent libertarians. The chapter concludes by proposing to look more deeply into the question of the anarchists' libertarianism. What needs asking, instead of whether the anarchists are consistent in espousing censure and liberty, is whether liberty really is their goal. This is the question that the succeeding chapter takes up.

THE CONCEPTUAL ARGUMENT

Political theorists often reconcile freedom and coercion with a conceptual argument, which claims, on the basis of what freedom means, that it is uncurtailed by some restraint. The will of God, the forces of the market and the commands of a revolutionary vanguard are famous examples of restraints that theorists have thus reconciled with freedom. In each case they have argued conceptually, if unconvincingly, that, because freedom as properly defined is unaffected by the restraint in question, the restraint, even though confining, leaves freedom uncurtailed.

The anarchists could use a conceptual argument of this type to prove that they are libertarians, if they defined freedom so that public censure did not obstruct it. In that case, the censorial restraints imposed in their good society, not counting as obstacles to liberty, could not consistently be cited to impugn it as their chief goal. Whether the anarchists can use this conceptual argument to vindicate their libertarianism thus depends on how they define freedom.

Like all concepts of freedom that apply to agents, the anarchists' is a triadic relation of *subjects* who are free from *restraints* to reach *objectives*.[3] No anarchist specifies all terms of this triad completely, but together they give it a thorough description.

Since what they say about the triad is for the most part consistent, their concept of liberty can be elucidated by treating their remarks about its various terms as complementary parts of a single whole.

Godwin and Bakunin are the clearest of the anarchists in describing the first term of the triad: the subject of freedom. For both of them it is the choices and actions of individuals that must be free. As Godwin says, a free man must not only act freely; in his prior deliberations he must 'consult his own reason, draw his own conclusions', 'exercise the powers of his understanding'. Bakunin makes the same point about the subject of liberty when he writes that no one is free 'unless all his actions are determined...by his own convictions'. And for Proudhon, 'one must think for oneself...to be free'.[4] According to the anarchists, then, it is not enough to act freely; one must also have freedom to decide.

As the foregoing quotations indicate, what makes decisions free for anarchists is their origin in rational deliberation. Free decisions, as anarchists conceive of them, are based on arguments and evidence that one has personally and systematically evaluated. Making the freedom of decisions depend on their arising from rational deliberation has implications for the second term of the triad, which identifies the restraints which leave freedom uncurtailed.

Rational deliberation is as much of a restraint on action and choice as more obvious forces, owing to its practical upshot. Anyone who deliberates rationally about the future draws conclusions from his reflections, and these conclusions restrict what he may choose or do. No one can successfully deliberate without encountering these restrictions, because they emerge unavoidably from deliberative activity. This fact shows the anarchists which restraints to identify as compatible with freedom. Recognizing that rational deliberation is restrictive, and believing it indispensable for freedom, the anarchists must conclude that the rational restraints that a deliberating agent imposes on himself do not obstruct his liberty. They must also accept the converse of this conclusion. Since rational deliberation is indispensable for liberty, restraints that directly hinder action and choice are not the only

ones that curtail freedom; restraints that hinder rational deliberation indirectly curtail it.

Proudhon is the most systematic of the anarchists in compiling
a list of the restraints which anarchists regard as hindrances to
free deliberation, choice and conduct. His list can therefore serve
most usefully to complete the description of their triad's second
term. Most lists of obstacles to the freedom of agents refer only to
those that humans deliberately impose or leave in place.[5]
Proudhon's list is more comprehensive. Not only 'the priest's
voice', 'the prince's order', and 'the crowd's cries' obstruct free
action, choice, and deliberation. Liberty, as 'the spirit of revolt',
recognizes 'no law, no argument, no authority, no end, no limit,
no principle, no purpose beyond itself'.[6] Proudhon is here extending a theme foreshadowed by Godwin and repeated by the later
anarchists: a free agent is liberated from every hindrance that can
be removed or lessened, except those arising from his own
deliberations.

The third term in the triad specifies the objectives of liberty:
what agents must be free to choose or do. The anarchists' description of this term is fixed by what they say about the others.
Having stated that freedom requires liberation from all but
rational impediments, they cannot put other limits on the goals
free persons may reach. We count as free for anarchists, whatever
we choose or do, provided that our choice and conduct are
rationally based. The agreement of the anarchists about the goal
of freedom gives the third term of their concept the unity it needs
to make their entire view of liberty coherent.

The analysis of freedom provided by the anarchists would
warrant viewing them as seeking liberty above all else, only if it
implied that the public censure they prescribe does not coerce.
Public censure, for the anarchists, involves 'a promptness to
enquire into and to judge' your neighbors' conduct.[7] Where this
sort of censure is common practice, behavior is controlled in three
different ways. It is controlled by penalties, in the form of
threatened or actual rebuke, which compel obedience from fear.
It is controlled by internalization, a process through which
censured individuals absorb prevalent standards of conduct. And

it is controlled with reasoned arguments, through whi[
censurer tries to convince his neighbors that they should [
their ways. Now certainly the rebuke which this complex censure
imposes curtails the anarchists' sort of freedom, because rebuke,
even if it is mild and private, still, as a penalty, hinders deliberation, choice and conduct. No doubt the anarchists could have
conceptually ruled out censorial rebuke as an interference with
liberty by explicitly classifying it as non-coercive, but they sensibly
avoided such an arbitrary fiat. Their comprehensive list of
obstacles to freedom contains no exception in favor of rebuke.
Since the meaning of freedom which the anarchists derive from
their analysis is too broad to reconcile it with censure, they can
only hope to achieve this reconciliation non-conceptually.

THE CRUDE EMPIRICAL ARGUMENTS

The anarchists have two kinds of empirical arguments, crude and
sophisticated, that might reconcile their use of censure with the
view that freedom is their chief aim. Both kinds of arguments
attempt to show that though it is conceptually possible for public
censure to curtail freedom, under anarchy this curtailment does
not occur. The crude empirical arguments claim that anarchist
censure, in its effects on freedom, is no hindrance at all. The
sophisticated arguments, while conceding that censure interferes
with freedom somewhat, see it as maximizing freedom on the
whole.

Godwin advances the crude argument in its boldest form by
claiming that anarchist censure increases freedom. A person's
freedom is curtailed, 'when he is restrained from acting upon the
dictates of his understanding'. Anarchist censure does not impose
this kind of restraint. It influences us in the same way as our
reading, through 'reasons. . .presented to the understanding',
which help us deliberate more rationally by suggesting arguments
and evidence we would overlook, if we decided alone. The
'rational restraint of public inspection', being an aid to deliberation, far from hindering freedom, lends it support.[8]

This version of the crude argument is appealing in its boldness, but though not entirely misguided, it fails to yield Godwin's conclusion. Anarchist censure *may* rationalize deliberation, but need not. Its effect on the rationality of deliberation depends on how people respond to it. If they use the arguments and evidence it presents to help them make decisions, then censure enables them to deliberate more rationally than they could alone. But, as noted earlier, anarchist censure does more than offer arguments and evidence: it also imposes sanctions, ranging from mild stigma to complete ostracism. In so far as fear of these sanctions inhibits the deliberative process, or deters adherence to its conclusions, the public censure prescribed by anarchists can hardly be called an aid to liberty.

Godwin is especially vulnerable to this objection, because he relies more obviously than most anarchists on censorial sanctions. A writer who describes censure under anarchy as 'a species of coercion' which 'carries despair to the mind' is in no position to claim that it is liberating.[9] But this claim holds up no better if ascribed to other anarchists since they all rely somewhat on condemnation and rebuke. Hence if the crude empirical argument is to serve the anarchists as proof that freedom is their chief goal, they must give it a more modest form than Godwin does, by showing that even though censure need not increase freedom, at least it leaves it uncurtailed.

Proudhon and Bakunin try to show this by appealing to the process of internalization, through which the directives issued by public opinion are absorbed by the individual and become part of his own frame of mind. They both see that these directives 'envelop us, penetrate us and regulate all of our movements, thoughts and actions'.[10] Bakunin thinks this process is so powerful that man is 'nothing but the product of society'.[11] Proudhon's view is more nuanced, since he gives more place in his social psychology to innate dispositions. But he agrees with Bakunin that conduct is guided to a considerable extent by internalized directives.

Proudhon and Bakunin go on to claim that because the directives issued by anarchist censure are internalized, they leave participants in anarchy free. Freedom can only be curtailed by 'an external master, a legislator, who is located outside of the person he commands'.[12] But the directives issued by censure, being internalized from opinion, 'are not imposed by an external legislator; . . .they are immanent in us, inherent, they constitute the very basis of our being; . . .hence instead of finding limits in them, we should consider them as the real conditions and the necessary foundation of our freedom'.[13] Censure does not restrict the freedom of an individual, because when he complies with it, his directive is a self-imposed 'secret commandment from himself to himself'.[14]

This argument fails, partly because, like Godwin's claim that censure rationalizes deliberation, it overlooks the reality of censorial sanctions. Anarchist censure is not perfectly internalized, but also controls externally by forcing individuals by means of rebuke to comply against their will. This censorial rebuke is obviously a bar to freedom, because it obstructs action, choice and deliberation just as decisively as any other kind of sanction. The anarchists could ignore the interference with liberty caused by rebuke, if in their good society it was not imposed. But since it is imposed there, they are unconvincing when they claim that because their censure is entirely internalized, it is coercionless.

But even if the anarchists eschewed rebuke entirely and relied on nothing but internalized censure, it still would obstruct their freedom. To count as free for anarchists, one must decide what to do on the basis of one's own rationally reached conclusions. Any other basis for choice interferes with liberty by blocking or bypassing deliberation. Now internalization, as described by anarchists, is not a rational process. Persons who internalize censorial directives unwittingly absorb them and then use them to decide without subjecting them to scrutiny.[15] Internalization, thus being a substitute for rational deliberation, and even a bar to it, is not a process that anarchists can deem coercionless. The directives issued by internalized censure may be self-imposed, but for anarchists this does not prevent them from coercing. For it is not just the internal origin, but also the rationality of the directives which determine choice that anarchists must consider in deciding if they curtail liberty. Since internalized censorial directives, though self-imposed, are not products of rational deliberation, anarchists, to be consistent, must admit that they coerce.

There is one other crude empirical argument in anarchist theory for the compatibility of freedom and public censure. This argument sees the restraint imposed by censure in a state of anarchy as unavoidable and hence as no more of a coercion than other restraints which cannot be overcome, such as that of mortality. Bakunin views censure in this light when he describes it as 'one of the conditions of social life against which revolt would be as useless as it would be impossible'.[16] The other anarchists agree (though less emphatically) that, owing to its inescapability, censure is coercionless.[17]

One might admit that, if censure under anarchy is really inescapable, it does not interfere with freedom. But why should it be viewed as beyond escape? Bakunin answers that it is needed for the survival of the self. 'A man is only himself insofar as he is a product' of society and 'has no existence except by virtue of its laws. Resistance to it would therefore be a ridiculous endeavor, a revolt against himself, a veritable suicide.'[18] Anarchist censure is inescapable for Bakunin because he thinks that anyone who is not restrained by it will lose his self.

It is true that humans, whose selves are formed through interaction, need the restraint of social influence to achieve identity. But this does not mean that they must be restrained by censure, a special kind of social influence, distinguished by being imposed deliberately: the censurer sets out with full awareness to correct his neighbor's conduct. Deliberate restraint of this sort is not needed to achieve identity, because the spontaneous pressures that members of all societies unintentionally exert on one another are sufficient to make each aware that he and all the others are distinct. Since identity can emerge without the help of censure, in an anarchist society as in any other, Bakunin's claim that it is inescapable is incorrect.

But even if censure was needed to *achieve* identity, it still would not be inescapable, unless it was also needed to *preserve* the self. For if the self could be preserved without the aid of censure, a developed individual would not have to submit to it. Now a developed individual who is unrestrained by censure need not lose his identity, because he can maintain it without submitting at all to social influence. While social influence is needed to form the self, the self once formed no longer depends on it for its existence, as its survival in isolated marooned sailors is enough to show. Since developed individuals can maintain identity without submitting to any social influence, they can certainly maintain it without submitting to censure.

These objections to Bakunin's claim that censure is beyond escape show that his version of the crude empirical argument for reconciling it with liberty is no more effective than those the other anarchists advance. But perhaps empirical arguments which are more sophisticated can show that censure and liberty accord.

THE SOPHISTICATED EMPIRICAL ARGUMENTS

The crude empirical arguments fail because they refuse to admit that anarchist censure *does* interfere with freedom. Denying this, they face the impossible task of explaining away its interference as rational, internal, or inescapable. The sophisticated empirical arguments are stronger than the crude ones because, by taking censure's interference with freedom into account, they can pose the problem of reconciliation more manageably. They need not show that censure leaves liberty uncurtailed, but only that it curtails liberty less than the alternatives do. If the sophisticated arguments could show this, they would not prove anarchists libertarian in the usual sense of seeking freedom above all else. But they would prove them libertarian in the sense of showing, whatever their objective, how the most freedom can be attained. Reliance on public censure would stand revealed as the best available aid to liberation.

The anarchists make no attempt to vindicate censure as more liberating than all other methods of behavioral control. Their strategy is to show only that it is more liberating than legal government, which they quite sensibly regard as the most plausible alternative. They argue that censure differs from legal government in ways which make it less coercive on the whole.

Legal government is a method of control marked by the following features: it is applied by a small number of officials, who issue general, standing rules to all members of society and who enforce these rules with fixed penalties for each type of offense.[19] All the comparable features of censure, as anarchists conceive of it, are different from those of legal government. Anarchist censure is applied by all members of society, rather than by a few officials. It issues changeable, particular imperatives, not permanent, general rules. It does not rely on fixed penalties to enforce these imperatives, but uses flexible sanctions, internalization and reasoned arguments.[20] Each of the features of legal government that distinguishes it from the anarchists' censure is blamed by them for making it more coercive.

The first of these features is remoteness. Legal government relies on a small group of officials to control conduct, whereas censorship relies on society at large. Being few in number, government officials lack the information about the attitudes and circumstances of their numerous subjects that is needed to control them as individuals, and hence must control them as an undifferentiated group. Censurers, on the other hand, being socially intimate with one another, can adjust their directives and sanctions to the situation of each individual so that, while still being effective, they interfere less with conduct.[21]

Even if legal government could be intimate, as might be possible in a small direct democracy, anarchists would still rate it as less liberating, partly because it must still control its subjects with general rules. However intimate a legal government may be, it works through laws, which, being general, require a whole class of persons to behave the same way in a wide range of cases. Censure, on the other hand, using singular imperatives, which prescribe 'not according to certain maxims previously written, but according to the circumstances of each particular cause', can better protect each subject's liberty.[22] The generality of legal rules makes government less liberating than censure by causing it to control behavior more indiscriminately.

The permanence of laws as well as their generality makes even the most intimate legal government less liberating than censure. It is because laws depend more than censorial directives on being publicly known that they must be more permanent. No law can be effective, unless those whom it controls know, before engaging in the activities it regulates, what behavior it requires or forbids. Censorial directives, on the other hand, being applied *ad hoc*, can effectively regulate behavior even if they are not known in advance. Laws must persist longer than censorial directives, because, if they change as often, the public cannot know what they say. The greater permanence of laws makes legal government less adjustable than censure to changing circumstances, just as their greater generality makes it less adjustable to particular circumstances. While the directives issued by censure can be easily modified so that they do not become more restrictive as conditions change, those issued by government have 'a tendency to crystallize what should be modified and developed day by day'.[23] The permanence of legal directives inhibits them from changing in new situations so as to minimize interference with free conduct at all times.

The same uniformity and permanence that make the directives issued by government more coercive than those of censure also make its sanctions more coercive. Governmental sanctions are uniform and fixed, because, being legal, they impose similar penalties for similar offenses.[24] Censorial sanctions can be more flexible, because they can impose different penalties for similar offenses, whether committed by different individuals, or by the same individual at different times. Now the same penalty is not needed to enforce a directive in every case. The attitudes and circumstances of some individuals are such that only mild coercion is needed to secure their compliance with many directives, while the same directives will be disobeyed by differently situated individuals, unless enforced by severe coercion. Hence governmental sanctions, being fixed and uniform, interfere substantially with conduct whether they are mild or severe. If an official enforces a directive with mild coercion, the widespread disobedience he allows impedes free action, while he directly impedes free action

19

if he enforces the directive with severe coercion. A censurer, on the other hand, not having to use uniform, fixed sanctions, can adjust his applications of rebuke so that they coerce each individual just enough to secure compliance. It is thus because censorial rebuke can coerce more economically than legal penalties can that anarchists consider it more liberating.

The anarchists are on firm ground in claiming that the remoteness of its officials and the general, permanent character of its controls make legal government harsher, and to that extent less liberating, than censure. But the same features of legal government which detract from its power to liberate by making its restraints on action harsh, contribute to its power to liberate by making them predictable.

The remoteness of government officials prevents them from effectively regulating behavior, except with predictable controls. Unpredictable controls would not be effective, because officials are too distant from their subjects to instruct them continually and individually about what they must do. The generality and permanence of legal controls give them just the sort of predictability that remote officials need.

Being general and permanent, legal directives set standing conditions under which broad classes of action are forbidden or enjoined. Legal sanctions, also being general and permanent, establish fixed penalties for each type of offense. Hence anyone subject to a legal government can know before he acts what conduct it requires of him and what penalty he will receive from it for disobedience. He can be sure that his conduct will not be hindered by his government, so long as he does what it prescribes.

Censure is less predictable, because its lack of generality and permanence makes it hard to know its requirements in advance. Censure prescribes different conduct for numerous particular situations that law treats as the same, and it prevents transgressions not with settled penalties for each offense, but with varying applications of rebuke. Hence persons subject to public censure, unsure what it will require and uncertain what it will do if they disobey, are less safe from the restraints it imposes on their action than from the restraints imposed on it by law. Even though the particularity and flexibility of censure make it a milder restraint than legal government, these characteristics need not make it less coercive. For besides making it milder, they also make it more unpredictable. Censorial restraint may be milder, but its greater unpredictability offsets the advantage for securing liberty that its mildness gives it as compared to law.

If remoteness, generality and permanence were all that distinguished legal government from censure, the anarchist case for rating it as more liberating would be inconclusive. But anarchist censure, unlike legal government, does not rely on sanctions alone to secure compliance with directives; it also uses internalization and reasoned argument. The anarchists point to both of these distinctive methods of enforcement as attributes that make censure less coercive.

So far as censure enforces its mandates with internalization, it impedes conduct less than government does. Sanctioned directives interfere with conduct, because their threats and penalties limit an individual's range of permissible acts. But internalized directives, not being enforced by threats and penalties, leave individuals free to act just as they please. The conduct of an individual is always restrained, so far as it is controlled by sanctions, but it is not restrained at all so far as it is controlled by internalization.

While this argument shows that internalization, by leaving action unrestrained, is more liberating for conduct than sanctions are, it does not show that internalization is more liberating on the whole. For the advantage of internalization over sanctions as a liberator, arising from its tolerance for conduct, is offset by its interference with thought. Sanctions do not interfere with thought, because they control what people do, not what they think. A person who follows a directive from fear of sanctions can think what he pleases about the merit of the action he carries out. But a person who follows an internalized directive is made to view his action as correct, because internalization controls its mental antecedents, the beliefs and intentions on which it rests. The restraint imposed on thought by internalization makes it no less of an impediment to the liberty of the anarchists than sanctions are, even though it is no impediment to action. For liberty, as conceived by anarchists, requires not only free action, but free thought.

The other method for enforcing directives, besides internalization, that distinguishes censure from government is reasoned argument. By claiming that censure tends more than government to win compliance with reasons, anarchists give themselves the hope, not offered by their other arguments, of proving their society libertarian. For it is a sound argument that, so far as censure differs from legal government by securing obedience with reasons, it serves freedom better.

The argument rests on the conceptual thesis of the anarchists examined earlier, which states that the conclusions an agent draws from his deliberations about the merit of his contemplated acts do not obstruct his liberty. This thesis allows the anarchists to argue that so far as censure secures obedience by giving reasons, it exercises coercionless control, by convincing its subjects to conclude from their own deliberations that the conduct it demands of them is right.

So far as censure secures obedience with sanctions as severe as legal government's, it is no more liberating, because equally severe sanctions, whether legal or censorial, whether they cause physical or mental suffering, impede deliberation to the same extent.[25] Anyone who complies with a directive from fear of sanctions is free to deliberate about the merit of the conduct it prescribes. He may even conclude that the act is wrong for him to do. But he does it anyway, because the sanction that controls him prevents him from following his conclusion by overpowering it with fear. Since sanctions, though they allow deliberation, deprive it of effect, they fail to control an agent through his own deliberations and so cannot be regarded by anarchists as leaving him free.

Reasoned argument differs from sanctions as a means to secure obedience by providing just the sort of restraint that a libertarian anarchy needs. The only situation in which an agent who is made to follow a directive bases his compliance on his own deliberations is where he is convinced by those who issue the directive that what they bid him to do is right. Since anarchist censure is distinguished from government by its greater tendency to give reasons of this kind, and since anarchists think a controlling agency must give such reasons in order to respect freedom, they are warranted in arguing that, so far as censure provides more of them than legal government does, it is the more liberating method of control.

Bakunin presents a clear version of this argument when he distinguishes government from censure on the ground that 'its nature is not to convince but to impose and to force'. The liberty of a man 'consists precisely in this: he does what is good not because he is commanded to, but because he understands it, wants it and loves it'. Government, which coerces its subjects with commands instead of convincing them with reasons, he therefore denounces as 'the legal violator of men's wills, the permanent negator of their liberty'.[26] No other anarchist makes this argument as forthrightly as Bakunin; but they all do make it, as they must, if their reconciliation of censure with freedom is possibly to succeed.[27] For of the many arguments they can or do advance to achieve this reconciliation, only this one hits the mark. Whether it is strong enough to prove anarchy libertarian is an issue that still must be assessed.

THE LIBERTARIANISM OF ANARCHIST CENSURE

Though only one of the sophisticated arguments supports the claim that anarchist censure is more liberating than legal government, they all bear on this claim's validity. For together they identify all of the features of anarchist censure that affect how well it protects freedom. These arguments reveal that its unpredictability and its interference with thought, through internalization, handicap anarchist censure as a liberator as compared to legal government. Hence it can only qualify as more liberating if it has the means to overcome these handicaps. Its greater ability to give reasons for obedience is its most powerful means for overcoming them. But it has other resources. Its mildness tends to offset its unpredictability. Its internality, which makes it

23

tolerant toward action, compensates to some extent for its control of thought. Hence the task of making it more liberating than government does not rest on its ability to give reasons alone. If anarchist censure, by giving reasons, offsets that portion of its disadvantage for achieving freedom that its mildness and internality do not overcome, the claim that it is more liberating than legal government is confirmed. But if, despite its greater tendency to give reasons, anarchist censure still interferes with freedom more, the claim that it is more liberating must be rejected.

These remarks show that a verdict on whether anarchy is more liberating than legal government requires an assessment of the extent to which it uses reasoned argument to control behavior. The next chapter makes this assessment by tracing out the implications for the rationality of anarchist censure of the communal individuality which, rather than freedom, it will be argued, is the anarchists' chief objective. Since the analysis that follows of the scope of liberty in an anarchist society proceeds from a fresh understanding of the goal which anarchists seek, and from a more accurate view than has previously been available of what they mean by censure, it promises finally to settle the dispute, begun by William Proby, whether anarchists are secret enemies of freedom, or loyal friends.

2

THE GOAL OF ANARCHISM:
COMMUNAL INDIVIDUALITY

The perplexing conjunction in anarchist theory of praise for freedom and use of an at least somewhat coercive censure has received varied explanations. To embarrassed friends of anarchism, such as George Woodcock, this conjunction is an oversight. 'Anarchists accept much too uncritically the idea of an active public opinion.' They 'have given insufficient thought to the danger of. . .the frown of the man next door becoming as much a thing to fear as the sentence of the judge'. Had they looked more closely into censure, Woodcock here implies, they would never have endorsed it, because they would then have found it too appalling. Henri Arvon, more detached in his view of anarchists, explains their espousal of both freedom and public censure as a quirk. Anarchists are guilty of a 'strange *gageure*' in 'wishing to maintain individual autonomy while also imposing social discipline'. And the acerbic Marxist George Plekhanov, as part of his campaign to discredit anarchists, finds that in seeking liberty while using censure they are 'running away from an insurmountable logical difficulty'.[1]

These explanations for why anarchists espouse both liberty and a censure that is at least residually coercive, though plausible, are uninviting, because they impugn the integrity of anarchism as systematic thought. If any of them is valid, the conjunction by anarchists of praise for liberty with use of censure lacks theoretical support, for it cannot be warranted theoretically, as an oversight, a quirk, or a mistake. Before resorting to these discrediting explanations for the espousal by the anarchists of liberty and censure, the possibility of explaining it within the terms of their theory deserves to be explored. It is the thesis of this chapter that

25

not freedom but community and individuality are the anarchists' chief goals and that these goals require censure. In an anarchist society, where these goals are realized, liberty is necessary, to be sure, but so is censure. Censure and liberty, rather than being unreconcilable opposites, work as complements to merge the goals of anarchism into a single complex value, which it is apt to call communal individuality.

THE NORMATIVE STATUS OF INDIVIDUALITY AND COMMUNITY IN ANARCHIST THOUGHT

Individuality as conceived by anarchists consists of traits of character that mark a well-developed self. Anarchists disagree about the marks of individuality and on whether it is generic or unique. For Godwin and Proudhon individuality is generically defined as traits of personality, such as rationality and emotional sensitivity, which are characteristic of all mankind.[2] Bakunin shares this generic view of individuality, but he also sometimes sees it as personally defined, in a way more fully articulated by Kropotkin, who describes it as 'the full expansion. . .of what is original' in men, 'an infinite variety of capacities, temperaments and individual energies'.[3] The disagreement among anarchists concerning the particular marks of individuality means they do not all aim for the same specific kind. But since they all believe that individuality, however specified, involves growth of personality, there is no reason why, understood as self-development, it cannot be their aim.

The conceptions of community advanced by anarchists are just as various as their conceptions of individuality. For Godwin the model of a community is a conversation. For Proudhon and Bakunin it is a productive enterprise. Kropotkin's model of a community embraces not only productive enterprises, but every kind of cooperative association. The differences among these varied models of community are telling and cannot be ignored. They provide a basis for the scheme worked out in the next chapter for classifying anarchism into types. But the differences in the anarchists' conceptions of community must not obscure the similarities. Although the contexts in which anarchists see community as occurring are rather different, the relations they envisage among its members are much the same. Godwin describes the members of a community as engaged in a 'free and unrestrained opening of the soul', a 'reading of each other's minds'.[4] Each member of a Proudhonian community 'recognizes his own self in that of others'.[5] I cannot participate in the community Bakunin seeks without finding 'my personality reflected as if by numerous mirrors in the consciousness...of those who surround me'.[6] And the member of Kropotkin's community is immersed in 'the perception of his oneness with each human being'.[7] What these descriptions show about relations in an anarchist community is that they involve reciprocal awareness. Each member of such a community knows not only what the others think, but also that they know what he is thinking. Awareness in an anarchist community is reciprocal, because each understands his fellows as he understands himself.[8] Just as the theme of self-development unifies the anarchists' various conceptions of individuality, so does the theme of reciprocal awareness unify their conceptions of community. It is just as impossible to claim that anarchists all seek a particular form of community as that they all seek a particular form of individuality. But since they share the belief that community involves reciprocal awareness, community conceived as such awareness can be their common goal.

Individuality and community, understood as self-development and reciprocal awareness, are not merely possible goals of anarchism. They, and not freedom, are the goals anarchists really seek. The easiest way to show this is by tracing the normative relationship in anarchist theory between individuality, community, and freedom. The warm praise that anarchists give freedom makes it seem their chief aim. But examination of their writings shows that they actually treat it as subordinate. Freedom is prized by anarchists more as a means to individuality and community than as a final end.

Godwin and Proudhon explicitly subordinate freedom to individuality. 'To be free is a circumstance of little value' for Godwin, 'without the magnanimity, energy and firmness', which he associates with individuality; 'liberty is chiefly valuable as a means to procure and perpetuate this temper of mind'.[9] Freedom has the same subordinate place for Proudhon, since he too views it as an aid to self-development, rather than as an inherent good. 'I have not made *liberty* my motto, because liberty is an indefinite, absorbing force that may be crushed.' 'The function of liberty is to carry the individual beyond all influences, appetites and laws ...to give him what might be called a supernatural character.'[10] Bakunin and Kropotkin are less explicit about the normative relationship between freedom and individuality, but they certainly suggest that freedom is subordinate. Thus Bakunin praises liberty for enabling man to become 'his own creator', and Kropotkin portrays it as an historical source of 'individual originality'.[11] Neither says explicitly that individuality has more value. But by consigning freedom to the status of a means to individuality, they imply that it has lesser worth.

Freedom is also subordinated by the anarchists to community. Thus, although Proudhonian anarchy is to provide 'all the liberty one could want', it must also furnish 'something more important than liberty: sincere and reciprocal enlightenment'.[12] Bakunin likewise warns against giving freedom in an anarchy too high a place. It must not usurp 'the superior claim of solidarity, which is and will always remain the greatest source of social goods'.[13] And Kropotkin follows his predecessors in requiring that 'the liberty of the individual' in a state of anarchy 'be limited by...the necessity, which everyone feels, of finding cooperation, support and sympathy among his neighbors'.[14]

Since individuality and community take precedence over freedom as the final destination of the anarchists, they cannot be called libertarians in the usual sense of seeking freedom above all else. While freedom might be maximized in their good society, this cannot be because such maximization is their main intention. But before investigating whether anarchists, despite their non-libertarian intention, maximize liberty nonetheless, an issue of internal coherence in their thought must be faced. By committing themselves equally to individuality and community, anarchists raise doubts whether their chief aims are consistent. For, lacking a principle to adjudicate between individuality and community, how can they judge situations where the courses these norms prescribe conflict?[15]

To meet this objection anarchists deny the possibility of conflict; they view each of their aims as dependent on the other for its full achievement. Bakunin, for example, thinks that 'the infinite diversity of individuals is the very cause, the principal basis, of their solidarity' and that solidarity serves in turn as 'the mother of individuality'.[16] The other anarchists all more or less explicitly agree. For all of them communal awareness springs from developed individuality, and developed individuality depends in turn on a close-knit common life. For all of them, community and individuality, as they develop, intensify each other and coalesce.[17]

Anarchists do not merely assert that individuality and community are reinforcing; they give reasons for this claim. According to Godwin, individuality, in the form of mental independence, supports community by drawing people toward each other. It is 'the grand fascination, by which we lay hold of the hearts of our neighbors'.[18] An intellectually independent person is more appealing than a person with conventional ideas. The attraction others feel for him moves them to learn what he is thinking and to reveal their own states of mind. In a society where individuality of Godwin's sort is well developed, awareness is thus reciprocal, and community prevails. Bakunin, whose view of individuality is less generic than Godwin's, offers a different reason why it supports community. Developed individuals, for Bakunin, are distinctive: each has some characteristic(s) the others lack. This diversity draws them into 'a collective whole, in which each completes the others and has need of them'.[19] Being various in personality, developed individuals depend more on one another to satisfy their needs than do individuals with similar personalities. Their bonds of mutual dependence encourage developed individuals to explore each other's character and thus to experience communal awareness. Proudhon and Kropotkin make the same case for how individuality supports community, by appealing to the attraction and dependence among developed individuals as reasons why their mutual awareness is so intense.[20] But Kropotkin also has a different argument. Among the marks of individuality that he mentions are 'social inclinations and instincts of solidarity'.[21] Hence well-developed individuals, having sociable desires, are disposed toward communal existence. In the words of Marc Guyeau, admired by Kropotkin as 'unconsciously anarchist', such individuals 'live too much to live alone'. They harbor 'an expansive force, ever ready to break out of the narrow casing of the self'.[22]

The other side of the thesis that individuality and community are reinforcing is the claim that community supports individuality. Anarchists offer arguments for this aspect of their thesis too. One such argument, advanced by Kropotkin, is that reciprocal awareness is an element of individuality. Even so strong a personality as Goethe would have found that community enlarged his self. 'He would have lost none of his great personal poetry or philosophy', but he would 'have gained. . .a new aspect of the human genius. (Consider his joy in discovering mutual reliance!) His whole being and individuality having developed in this new direction. . . another string would have been added to his lyre.'[23] If community would have added to Goethe's personality, it can certainly add to selves of less developed persons.

In arguing for community as a support for individuality, anarchists claim it not only as a constituent of the self, but also as a cause of the self's growth. Thus Godwin holds that the reciprocity of awareness in a community elicits mutual trust, and that this trust encourages the growth of intellect. Participants in a community are confident enough to 'compare their ideas, suggest their doubts, examine their mutual difficulties' openly, all of which improve their understanding.[24] The reciprocity of awareness among members of a community is also seen by Godwin as causing emotional development. 'Emotions are scarcely ever thrilling and electrical, without something of social feeling.'[25] Since such feeling is intense in a community, it encourages emotional life to flourish.

The arguments of the anarchists for viewing individuality and community as reinforcing may suffice to rebut the objection that these goals must conflict. But it is one thing to show the consistency of the anarchists in seeking communal individuality, and another to show that they design their good society to achieve it. The main thesis of this chapter, which now must be defended, is that the anarchists' commitment to communal individuality *requires* them to introduce into their good society the strange amalgam of censure and liberty that is so usually thought a scandal.

LIBERTY, CENSURE AND INDIVIDUALITY

Though anarchists do not aim for liberty above all else, it is important to them as a means for reaching the goals they do seek. Liberty plays an especially important part for anarchists as a means to individuality. Several of them comment generally on how liberty fosters individuality, but Godwin best explains its utility for this purpose.[26] He points out that the intellectual independence associated by all anarchists with individuality requires freedom, being unachievable unless the thought and action of individuals are substantially unrestrained. Freedom is also needed to support the emotional element in individuality, which includes the capacity for strong and subtle feelings, and the will to express them. In an atmosphere of freedom 'the more delicate affections...have the time to expand themselves'.[27] Moreover, we then strongly desire to express these feelings, not only because they are powerful, but because our freedom makes their expression safe. 'Our thoughts and words', not 'beset on every side with penalty and menace', can be openly communicated.[28]

Freedom is not the only condition identified by anarchists as encouraging individuality. They also stress the need for public censure: to stimulate self-consciousness, to enrich personality, and to direct emotions into channels that are strengthening to the self. Godwin offers the clearest argument for the claim, upheld by several anarchists, that public censure, by stimulating self-consciousness, encourages individuality. 'We have never a strong feeling' for our traits of character, 'except so far as they are confirmed to us by the suffrage of our neighbors'. If no one sets out deliberately to tell me what he thinks of my conduct, I will have a weak self-image, because our sense of self depends 'upon the consent of other human understandings sanctioning the judgment of our own'.[29] Since I cannot be fully aware of myself as an individual without being subject to others' deliberate judgment, and since such judgment, if unfavorable, amounts to censure, censure is indispensable for individuality. No one can know himself completely as an individual unless he feels it.

The second way that censure supports individuality for the anarchists is by providing a rich store of the thoughts and feelings that are the materials from which the self develops. Persons subject to public censure encounter ideas and emotions with a vividness that they would miss in isolation, or even in a society where spontaneous social influence, rather than censure, prevails. These ideas and emotions are a mental treasure which they can draw on to enrich their personalities.[30]

The final and most subtle of the anarchists' arguments for the claim that censure encourages individuality concerns its effects on the emotions. Anarchists are anxious about the harm to self-development caused by uncontrolled emotions and believe that public censure can prevent it. A person unrestrained by social influence cannot be an individual, says Bakunin, because without its help 'he cannot subordinate his instincts and the movements of his body to the direction of his mind'.[31] But social influence, whether spontaneous or deliberately applied as censure, is more than a restraint upon the passions, keeping them out of reason's way. Anyone affected by it, according to Proudhon, 'rids himself of his primitive savagery', to be sure. But he also develops his individuality. 'Without losing his animality, which he makes more delicate and beautiful, . . .he raises himself from a passion-ridden to a moral condition; . . .he enlarges his self, he augments and enlivens his faculties.'[32] Social influence and public censure are thus viewed by anarchists as helping us to cultivate our feelings. They help us grow as individuals by releasing us from the grip of confining emotions which they redirect into channels nourishing to an independent self.

By arguing that censure as well as liberty is needed for individuality, the anarchists require their good society to make use of both. This requirement would not restrict freedom in a state of anarchy if censure could sufficiently encourage individuality by giving reasons. But censure cannot support individuality in the ways envisioned by the anarchists by means of reasoned argument alone. It cannot stimulate self-consciousness in the persons it affects without sometimes rebuking, and thus coercively hindering, their conduct. It cannot enrich their personalities or cultivate their emotions without coercively permeating their minds. Since censure must issue penalties and be internalized in order to promote the anarchists' kind of individuality, it is bound to diminish their kind of freedom. Censure curtails freedom in a state of anarchy in order to make individuality flourish.

LIBERTY, CENSURE AND COMMUNITY

Anarchists argue that censure must curtail liberty not only to maximize individuality, but also to maximize community. One way that censure supports community, in their view, is by opening the opportunity to enter other minds. Reciprocal awareness cannot occur among people who conceal their sentiments, because guarded minds are closed to public view. But since censure involves the frank disclosure of opinions, those who engage in it gain at least the chance for the access to one another's consciousness on which the possibility of reciprocal consciousness depends.[33]

But even among people who express their sentiments, reciprocal awareness may be lacking, because they express them partially, or imprecisely, or because others misinterpret what they say. In none of these cases is their awareness mutual, because others understand them differently from the way they understand themselves. Accuracy in the disclosure and interpretation of thoughts and feelings is thus crucial to the anarchists for achieving their communitarian ideal. Public censure is one means they rely on to secure these kinds of accuracy.

Since persons who censure one another express their opinions with unusual candor, they are remarkably able to note discrepancies between their own words and thoughts. Their awareness of these discrepancies not only helps correct them: it also makes them difficult to maintain. For the only way knowingly to maintain a difference between what one thinks and what one says is by deliberate deception, which calls for 'great mastery in the arts of ambiguity and evasion, and such a perfect command of countenance as shall prevent it from being an index to our real sentiments'.[34] Such deception is always difficult. In a society which practices censure it is virtually impossible, because each member of such a society is under others' constant scrutiny. Nor is it likely that, in such a society, expressions of opinion will be misread. Since each can rely on others to communicate accurately, there is small need to interpret what they say. The confidence engendered among persons who treat each other honestly encourages community by making generally available an accurate expression of each individual's sentiments.

As for how liberty contributes to community, anarchists see it as both an indirect support, encouraging traits of character which in turn aid mutual awareness, and as a direct support. Rationality is perhaps the most salient of the character traits beneficial to community which anarchists, using the usual liberal arguments for free expression, see as nurtured by freedom. Their argument for how liberty directly supports community is less familiar. No matter how forthright I may wish to be, I cannot enter into relations of mutual awareness if my thought or (communicative) action is too restrained. For, to the extent that they are impeded, I am kept from knowing others' sentiments or expressing my own. Understanding this, anarchists value free expression not only as aiding rationality, but also on the ground, too often overlooked, that it opens the way to communal relations. Awareness tends to grow more mutual when people enjoy liberty to think and speak.[35]

But while anarchists see that freedom helps attain community, they also see that freedom, in order to help attain it, must be limited by censure. For if censure is to support community by opening minds and preventing deceit, it must interfere somewhat with freedom of expression. Thus the anarchists' perplexing espousal of both censure and freedom is explained as much by their desire for community as by their desire for individuality.

Censure, for the anarchists, can foster neither of these objectives unless conjoined with freedom; and freedom can only foster them when censure is imposed on it as a restraint.

HOW FREE IS ANARCHY?

Once it is recognized that the anarchists' chief aim is communal individuality, the previously unsettled issue, whether anarchy or legal government is more liberating, can be resolved. For the fact that anarchists aim for communal individuality does more than explain why their good society makes use of censure: it also suggests how to measure, more accurately than before, how much this censure curtails freedom. In a full-fledged anarchist society, where communal individuality is complete, the censure needed to prevent misbehavior allows more freedom than legal government does, because individuality and community both reduce the need for censure that is coercive. It will be remembered that of the three ways in which anarchist censure controls behavior, only its sanctions and internalization coerce. Now the censure imposed in an anarchist society, while working partially through sanctions and internalization, can work for the most part through the non-coercive giving of reasons, because the individuality and community that characterize such a society make control by rational censure unusually effective.

All the anarchists defend some version of the thesis that a developed individual is more amenable to reasoned argument, and more cooperative, than a person whose individuality is weak. Godwin, for whom individuality consists mainly in 'exercising the powers of...understanding', must believe that it opens us to the sway of reason.[36] What is less obvious is his belief that individuality fosters cooperation. A developed individual has 'a generous consciousness of [his] independence' which, far from isolating him, leads him to identify with others.[37] The later anarchists accept Godwin's point about individuality being rational, but do not stress it, being more concerned to elaborate his hint that individuality stimulates cooperation. Proudhon, for instance, dwells on how a person's concern for others deepens as he grows

35

more individual. Individuality is a 'feeling that overflows the self, and though intimate and immanent in our personality, seems to envelop it along with the personalities of all men'.[38] Kropotkin only elaborates on Proudhon when he describes the strong individual as 'overflowing with emotional and intellectual energy'. If your self is well developed, 'you will spread your intelligence, your love, your energy of action broadcast among others'.[39] Thus anarchist individuals, being unusually rational and cooperative, can be more readily controlled without coercion than persons whose individuality is weak.

The reciprocal awareness among the members of an anarchy, as well as their individuality, explains why reasoned argument so effectively controls their conduct. Where community is lacking, control must be more coercive because it is then more difficult to concert action voluntarily. Each person, unaware of others' sentiments or of what they think of him, regards his neighbors with a distrust that provokes deception and kindles hatred.[40] But where awareness is reciprocal, 'hatred would perish from a failure in its principal ingredient, the duplicity and impenetrableness of human actions'.[41] Reciprocity of consciousness elicits reciprocity of trust, which tends to develop into reciprocal benevolence.[42] The confidence and kindliness among members of an anarchist community encourage the same cooperative relations as their individuality. Being psychologically in touch with one another, participants in anarchy can regulate their conduct less with sanctions or internalization and more with reasons, than persons unconnected by communal ties.

Having examined the implications of the anarchists' objectives for the amount and type of censure in their regime, we can settle the issue left open in the previous chapter of whether anarchy or legal government is more liberating. The conclusion of that chapter was that anarchy is more liberating, if its censure is rational enough to compensate for the main sources of its greater coercion: the unpredictability of its sanctions and the interference of its internalization with thought. Now the burden of the analysis presented in this chapter is that the communal individuality which pervades anarchy diminishes the need to control behavior

How free is anarchy?

with unpredictable sanctions and internalized thought control. By engendering mutual trust, cooperative attitudes and susceptibility to arguments, it enables censure to achieve what little regulation of behavior is required mainly by giving reasons. Thus the individualizing communality of anarchist society makes it markedly freer than legal government, whose remote officials coerce more harshly with general, permanent laws.

This conclusion might be contested on the ground that legal government is perfectly compatible with individuality and community. Since these are the attributes that make anarchy more libertarian, a legal government that has them must be just as free.

If communal individuality under legal government could be as great as under anarchy, the claim that anarchy is more liberating might be false. But legal government suffers from disabilities which arrest communal individuality's growth. For one thing, it uses physical sanctions which, so far as they arouse more hostility and resentment than the psychological sanctions used by anarchy, impede the development of communal individuality more.[43] The characterizing traits of legal government compound the difficulty of developing communal individuality in its jurisdiction. The remoteness of its officials and the permanence and generality of its controls cause it to treat its subjects as abstract strangers. Such treatment is the very opposite of the personal friendly treatment under which communal individuality best grows.

But it would be unfair to rest the case for the greater freedom of an anarchy on a comparison between a fully developed anarchist society and a deficient legal government. If the anarchist is allowed an ideal setting in which to test the coerciveness of censure, then law must be put to the test in an equally well-developed legal society, where strong individuality, harmonious communality and great amenability to reason also reign. It is because communal individuality is so complete in an ideal anarchy that it can rely on reasoned argument to the near exclusion of coercive internalization and rebuke. Why could not the law, in a similarly ideal legal society, replace physical coercion with reasoned argument to a similar extent?

If the control exercised by legal government was not incurably

37

remote, permanent and general, perhaps it could do this. Its remoteness can certainly be appreciably diminished by increasing the proportion of officials to subjects and by bringing both groups into close contact. But since even officials who are intimate with their subjects must, in a legal government, control with laws, they are simply unable to enter very far into particularized face-to-face discussion with their subjects concerning the merit of specific acts. Legal government, to the extent that it gives reasons for obedience, addresses them to the merit of following its fixed, general rules. It argues that its dissenting subject, even if he deems a particular legally prescribed act harmful, should do it nonetheless, because of the value derived from its general performance. Since legal government is prevented by the inescapable generality and permanence of its controls from taking as much advantage as anarchy can of the potential offered by communal individuality for diminishing coercion through the giving of specific reasons, we must conclude that even when the two are compared on equally ideal grounds, anarchist society must be deemed more free.

Though the standard interpretation of the anarchists as libertarians is mistaken, it properly calls attention to the importance of freedom in their model of a good society. Where this interpretation goes wrong is in explaining freedom's importance for the anarchists as arising from its status as their chief value. The analysis of anarchist theory presented in this chapter shows how to make viewing it as libertarian acceptable. Though anarchists provide more freedom in their good society than legal government (the most promising alternative) provides, they do not set out to do so. They provide it, not as a pre-eminent good, but as a concomitant of the communal individuality that is their first concern. So long as freedom is recognized as being, for anarchists, a valued by-product of their search for communal individuality, there is no harm in describing them as libertarians. For their libertarianism then stands forth in its true light, as a libertarianism not of direct intention, but of oblique effect. Those who have followed William Proby in denouncing anarchists as freedom's secret enemies have been misguided, but not because freedom is the anarchists' most cherished good. Viewing anarchists as single-minded devotees of freedom is also erroneous. Anarchists are certainly not enemies of freedom, but their friendship is mediated and indirect.

This chapter has provided a general analysis of how anarchists think individuality and community are related. We have found their arguments persuasive for the claim that in an anarchy the reinforcing merger of these values maximizes freedom. But no general analysis can establish concretely how community and individuality merge for anarchists, because each anarchist would merge them somewhat differently. Hence the concreteness of anarchist theory, which, it will be remembered, is where it exceeds Marx's in promise, can only be appreciated through investigating the particular anarchists' diverse conceptions of this merger. Since each anarchist's conception is a modulated application of a general theory which all share, examining these conceptions will further clarify the structure of their thought. Learning how anarchists differ in their plans for communal individuality will give a more accurate grasp of their entire project.

3

VARIETIES OF ANARCHY

The anarchists' case for freedom would be flimsy if their way of maximizing individuality and community was only abstract. But they do more than show why abstract individuality and community are reinforcing. Each seeks a concrete individuality and community with mutual relations of a distinct type. Each traces the character of these relations, rejoicing in those that unite individuality and community, worrying about those that cause them to conflict. Finally, to relieve this worry, each anarchist introduces a mediating agent, a cohesive social attitude, to bind individuality and community firmly so that conflict between them is decreased. The elements of anarchy that most affect how well it nurtures freedom are thus the characters of its individuality, of its community and of the attitude it uses to encourage their accord.

There is disagreement among anarchists about the kind of individuality and community a well-ordered society creates. For the early anarchists, above all Godwin, community involves mainly rational awareness, and individuality has generic traits. For later anarchists, especially Kropotkin, communal ties are more emotional, and individuality lies less in what a person shares with others than in what makes him unique. Along with these shifts in the anarchists' conception of individuality and community go changes in the attitude they use to make individuality and community coalesce. Godwin relies on sincerity; Proudhon and Bakunin on respect; Kropotkin uses mutual benevolence. These differences among anarchists give their visions of a good society distinctive character. Godwin's anarchy, with its generic individuality, rational community and mediating sincerity, is like a thoughtful, candid conversation. For Proudhon and Bakunin, who favor somewhat more particular, emotional forms of individuality and community, and who mediate their conflicts with respect, anarchy resembles life among collaborators in a productive enterprise. Kropotkin's anarchy, which uses mutual benevolence to mediate between a highly personal individuality and a community marked by strong affective ties, is like an extended group of friendly neighbors.

Though characterizing anarchy as conversation, enterprise or neighborhood gives only a rough classification of types, it captures enough of the diversity within anarchism to make its expository use worthwhile. Seeing the types of anarchy as like one or another of these social patterns brings out salient differences, while confirming that all take the same ideal of communal individuality as their lodestar.

GODWIN: ANARCHY AS CONVERSATION

An individual, for Godwin, must be mentally independent, in the sense that he grounds his beliefs and actions on his own assessment of their merits. If others determine his acts or opinions for him, he is not an individual, because then his mind and theirs are indistinguishable. 'Following the train of his disquisitions and exercising the power of his understanding' makes a man an individual by differentiating him mentally from other people.[1] The mark of the Godwinian individual is thus generic reason. One finds individuality by sharing with others the capacity of the human species for independent thought.

Two misconceptions about Godwinian individuality must be set aside before its relation to community can be accurately assessed. For one thing, Godwin's emphatically rational individuality seems to be opposed to emotions. Not only does Godwin exclude emotions from the marks of individuality, he also sees them as a threat. To maintain individuality requires repressed feelings. We must resist the desire to 'indulge in the gratifications and cultivate the feelings of man' lest, resigning ourselves 'wholly to sympathy and imitation', we become intellectually dependent.[2]

But Godwin's hostility to emotions is not absolute. Without 'the genuine emotions of the heart' we are 'the mere shadows of men, . . .destitute of substance and soul'.[3] An emotionless person, though logically able to be an individual, will not become one. Feelings which encourage independent thinking are thus valued aids to individuality. Godwin wants to direct emotions, not expunge them.

There is also some apparent basis in Godwin's individuality for seeing it as endangered by community. The best evidence for this view is his attack on cooperation 'for imprisoning. . .the operation of our own mind'. How can Godwin think community aids individuals when he calls even the cooperation among actors and musicians 'absurd and vicious'?[4] Once one grasps that he attacks cooperation so far as it weakens individuals, and not as being bound to weaken them, his view of its effect on individuality is revealed to be nuanced. Concerts and dramas threaten individuals because they require 'formal repetition of other men's ideas'.[5] But cooperation encouraging to mental independence deserves praise. The opposition to community that Godwin's individuality provokes also leads to giving community qualified support.

The kind of community that Godwin sanctions occurs among participants in conversation. He admits that conversation, as a species of cooperation, involves 'one or the other party always yielding to have his ideas guided by the other'.[6] But conversers, unlike actors or musicians, suffer no interference when they cooperate with the independence of their minds. In fact, conversation serves individuality because the remarks of other parties, rather than imprisoning one's thoughts and feelings, help them grow. 'Conversation accustoms us to hear a variety of sentiments, obliges us to exercise patience and attention, and gives freedom and elasticity to our disquisitions.'[7] Not only does conversation encourage mental independence: by exposing us to new ideas, it gives that independence wider scope.

To explain better how conversation serves individuals, Godwin likens it to a mirror. Just as a mirror helps me know my physical identity, so conversation helps me know my mental self. Through his reactions to my statements, an interlocutor reflects them, so that I understand them better than I could alone. My firmer grasp of my expressed opinions helps me criticize them, so as to increase the independence of my thought.[8]

By comparing conversation to a mirror, Godwin clarifies his thesis that it creates individuals, but he also calls his thesis into doubt. For the figure of a mirror is most used by analysts to account for social emulation. When Rousseau explained conflict and conformity as arising from our desire to shine in others' eyes, he equipped social theory with a helpful tool, perhaps used most aptly by C. H. Cooley, in his discussion of the 'looking-glass self'. Cooley sees even more clearly than Rousseau that a man's socially reflected image, far from helping him become an independent thinker, makes him a copy of those with whom he interacts. The character of social men is so 'largely caught up from the persons they are with' that they always 'share the judgements of the other mind'.[9] How can Godwin think conversation favors individuality, when, as a form of interaction, it creates a social self?

It is in answering this question that Godwin calls attention to the individualizing aspects of sincerity, which for him consists in 'telling every man the truth, regardless of the dictates of worldly prudence and custom'.[10] He readily admits the harm for mental independence of conversation that is insincere. Since an insincere converser hides his sentiments, he cannot serve others as a mirror in which to reflect and clarify their ideas. He serves them as a mirror, to be sure, but one which, like Cooley's, is apt to reflect social expectations and so discourages the development of independent thought. To make matters worse, insincerity is contagious. When one converser hides his sentiments, so do the rest. And when none are candid, all benefit of conversation for individuality is lost. 'Reserve, deceitfulness and an artful exhibition of ourselves take from the human form its soul and leave us the unanimated semblance of what man might have been, of what he would have been, were not every impulse of the mind thus stunted and destroyed.'[11]

By tracing the harm of conversation for self-development to insincerity, rather than to the character of interaction, Godwin avoids concluding with sociologists like Cooley that conversation must cramp the self. So long as my interlocutor is deceptive, Godwin argues, he cannot help me be an individual. For I will conceal my thoughts from someone who may mock them secretly. But if he speaks sincerely, I have no need to hide my sentiments from fear. I will express them fully, thereby achieving mental independence, because his sincere response to my statements helps me more than a dishonest response does to evaluate them for myself.[12]

The sincerity of Godwinian conversation not only helps it create individuals, it also helps tie these individuals together. All conversation is to some degree communal because participants, having close, egalitarian relations, must be somewhat conscious of one another's minds. But where sincerity is lacking, notes Godwin, obstacles to mutual awareness arise. Insincerity, by fostering deceit among conversers, makes each eye the other 'as if he expected to receive from him a secret wound'.[13] By arousing uncertainty about how others view their thoughts, it produces 'zeal for proselytism and impatience of contradiction'.[14] And by masking character it breeds permissiveness and calumny. 'The basest hypocrite passes through life with applause; and the purest character is loaded with unmerited aspersions.'[15] Sincere conversers, on the other hand, being free of the suspicion, fear and hatred that insincerity excites, and hence less separated by practices like proselytism or libel, are better able to unite as a community. Furthermore, they seek communal contacts, for candor and forthrightness elicit their attention and make them eager to know one another's minds.[16]

How sincerity unites conversers in community is neatly captured by the figure of a mirror. One mark of a community is awareness that the other members know my thoughts. Only if they reflect my thinking can I have this awareness, for otherwise I lack the evidence on which it must be based. Now sincerity, by making individuals transparent, might seem to keep them from reflecting anything whatever, including other minds. For how can a transparent surface be a mirror? But what sincerity does, says Godwin, is strip off the social mask which obstructs communication so as to expose rational identity, the only kind one can rely on to reflect another self. It is thus precisely because sincerity makes us transparent on the surface that it lays bare the inner mirror which creates communal ties. Freed of the social pretenses that mask their rational selves, sincere conversers reflect the thoughts of others faithfully, so that mutual awareness grows intense.

The merit of Godwin's reliance on sincere conversation, in which all participants disclose their true beliefs, to mediate between community and individuality turns on the answers to three questions: Is sincerity achievable? Is it effective as a mediator? Is it a valuable social trait?

The most radical argument for rejecting Godwin's sincerity as unachievable, made familiar by the French moralists, claims that the self-watching it requires is self-defeating. Godwin's sincerity is a consciously willed condition, reached by watching and changing one's state of mind. Now this sort of deliberate self-observation interferes with the candor it is intended to achieve. The sentiments of one who tries to be sincere are disingenuous because they are transformed by being watched into 'a cerebral invention, a kind of posturing'.[17]

This objection to sincerity counts heavily against those versions which emphasize ingenuous emotions. But Godwin's version is more rational. Sincerity for him requires full disclosure of opinions and beliefs, so far as they result from rational deliberation; but emotions, being significant above all as deliberative aids, may sometimes be legitimately concealed.[18] The very self-watching which complicates the search for emotional sincerity thus helps achieve the more rational Godwinian kind. For while self-watching harms the spontaneity of feelings, it helps give a reasoned grounding to beliefs.

Godwin cannot so easily escape other arguments for calling sincerity unreachable which deny the possibility of candid thought. Perhaps the most interesting of these arguments points to the effect of sincerity on shadowy or tentative ideas. Instead of disclosing ideas which are uncertain, sincerity distorts them by making them seem too firm and definite. It is self-defeating because it exposes secret thoughts to too much light.[19]

To this objection Godwin can respond in the same way as to the first one: by pointing out how limited his sincerity is in scope.

Not all our thoughts need be revealed for us to share Godwinian sincerity. What it requires is disclosure of rational beliefs. Since sincerity for Godwin applies to rational beliefs, whose clarity permits their accurate disclosure, rather than to tentative or secret thoughts, which when disclosed become distorted, it is narrow enough in scope to be achievable.

A final ground for calling sincerity unreachable, more modest than the foregoing, claims not that it is self-defeating but that, owing to discrepancies between thought and expression, it cannot be entirely achieved. No method of communication transmits even rational beliefs with perfect accuracy, since they are too numerous for all to be expressed. Furthermore, our gestures, speech and writing use standardized conventions, which schematize communicated thought. Rational beliefs defy exposure, because our power to express them is too weak.[20]

While admitting the force of this objection, Godwin regards it as innocuous, so far as his reliance on sincerity to mediate between individuals and their community is concerned. Such mediation is accomplished best by that sincerity which supports reciprocal awareness and independent thought the most. Perfect sincerity, which for Godwin means disclosing all rational beliefs, is not well suited for such mediating, since individuality and community are sometimes damaged by too much disclosure of even reasoned thought. If I withhold or temper my reasoned finding that an interlocutor is a fool, I diminish my sincerity but help reach the end it is meant to serve. 'Sincerity is only a means.' 'The man who thinks only how to preserve his sincerity is a glaringly imperfect character.'[21] Since Godwin does not seek complete sincerity, he can easily accept the argument that it must be incomplete.

Even if sincerity is reachable to the extent that Godwin hopes, it still would fail to serve him as a mediator unless it helps create communally related individuals. Thoughtful examiners of sincerity have usually denied that it can do this. Nietzsche was not the last to warn against sincerity as intrusive to the self. He sees self-development as a secret process, involving 'delicate decisions'. An individual is 'a concealed one, who instinctively uses speech for silence and withholding. . .and encourages a mask of himself to wander about in the hearts and minds of his friends'.[22] For Santayana, as for Nietzsche, individuals need masks, though less to guard the self than to define its character. In assuming a visage, 'we encourage ourselves eloquently to be what we are. . .We wrap ourselves gracefully in the mantle of our inalienable part.'[23] These themes are now standard among observers of sincerity, who routinely note how masks protect and shape the self.[24]

If sincerity harms individuals, it indirectly harms Godwinian community which has individuals for components. But writers on sincerity also find it harms community by directly blocking mutual awareness. André Gide, for instance, thinks sincerity 'can only concern those who have nothing to say'. Sincere ones, says Gide, are so absorbed by introspection that they can't communicate.[25] George Simmel sees sincerity as impeding mutual awareness by making others less attractive. 'Portions even of the persons closest to us must be offered us in the form of indistinctness and unclarity, in order for their attractiveness to keep on the same high level.'[26]

To meet these objections to his reliance on sincerity as a mediator, Godwin can appeal again to the rational character of the individuality and community he uses sincerity to help reach. It is our ability to develop and share delicate emotions, transient perceptions, elusive intimations that is most threatened by stark frankness. Sincerity is less harmful to the more solid and permanent – because rationally grounded – sentiments that define and unite Godwinian individuals. Nevertheless, sincerity might plausibly be charged with harming even Godwin's communal individuality, were it not for the conversational context in which it occurs. The objections to sincerity just considered all take as their context the existing social order with its opaque impersonality. There indeed 'complete openness would encounter misunderstanding, inability to forgive, limited tolerance for differences'. It might even be 'the greatest threat to civilized social life'.[27] But the close, egalitarian connections among participants in conversation dispel the mistrust that makes achieving communal individuality through frank disclosure difficult. The conversational context of Godwin's good society works in tandem with its rationality to help sincerity join its members in community.

The final question which affects the merit of sincere conversation, as Godwin uses it, is its value as a social trait. For sincerity, though attainable and an effective mediator between individuality and community, still might cause outweighing harm. The harm that sincerity can be most plausibly charged with causing is to privacy. When sincerity is practiced, privacy declines, because the barriers between myself and others, which keep them from observing me, are breached. To the extent, then, that privacy has value, sincerity is suspect.

Statements can be found in Godwin which suggest he answers this objection by denying that privacy has worth. For he berates 'the solitary anchorite' as parasitical, and his ideal society would be one whose member 'had no hopes in concealment [and] saw at every turn that the eye of the world was upon him'.[28] But Godwin does not oppose all forms of privacy, just those based on indifference or reserve. If I escape observation because others are uncaring, or because I hide my thoughts, Godwin does think privacy lacks value. But if my privacy results from solitude or discretion, as when I withdraw from interaction or count on others not to probe or spy, then for Godwin my privacy has worth.[29]

By drawing this distinction, Godwin enables himself to assure candor, while also protecting private life. As conversationalists, the members of his anarchy are open and sincere because they care about each other and disclose their beliefs. But they also have a private life, being discreet in conversation and at home in solitude. The sincerity of frank disclosure is thus limited in Godwin's anarchy by barriers of discretion and islands of seclusion to save privacy.

Godwinian sincerity emerges from this survey of objections as defensible in the role assigned to it. Being limited in scope by its rational character, in range of application by its conversational context, and in operation by its respect for privacy, it is an appropriate mediator between the commensurately limited self-development and reciprocal awareness it is designed to help secure. For Godwin's successors, however, who seek a more extensive communal individuality, sincerity has too many traps to be their mediator. They need a substitute that melds the more particularized individuals they search for into the more embracing community it is their purpose to achieve.

PROUDHON AND BAKUNIN:
ANARCHY AS A PRODUCTIVE ENTERPRISE

The close agreement between Proudhon and Bakunin concerning individuality, community and how to mediate between them justifies considering their plans for anarchy together. Certainly their plans have differences, but Bakunin, an avowed disciple of Proudhon, agrees with him on basic points of social structure.

Rationality marks developed individuals as much for Proudhon and Bakunin as for Godwin.[30] Where they differ from their predecessor in their view of individuality is in finding other signs of the developed self. Emotional vitality, which merely aids self-development for Godwin, is one such sign.[31] Another is the capacity for productive work, in which Proudhon and Bakunin see such individualizing qualities as 'bodily strength, manual dexterity, mental quickness, intellectual energy, pride in having overcome difficulties, mastered nature, acquired knowledge, gained independence'.[32]

By identifying three aspects of individuality rather than one, as Godwin had, Proudhon and Bakunin give their vision of self-development more richness, but they also make it harder to achieve. For it is surely harder to be rational, emotional and productive, than to be rational alone. One way they meet this problem is by arguing that productive work aids rationality, being its major source. Through making things, we test beliefs and discover facts. Hence one whose individuality is productive is more apt to engage in reasoned thought.[33]

To show that the emotional element of individuality can be achieved together with its productive and rational elements, Proudhon and Bakunin use a different argument. Rather than

49

viewing emotionality as arising from one of the other aspects of individuality, they claim that, though its source is independent, it has to develop, for individuality as a whole to be complete. 'The mind is troubled', writes Proudhon, 'if any one faculty tries to usurp power.' 'The opposition of faculties, their mutual reaction, is the source of mental equilibrium.'[34] Unless emotions have the strength to counter the mind's rational and productive tendencies, none will reach complete development. The individuality sought by Proudhon and Bakunin thus differs from the kind that Godwin seeks, not only in having several elements, but in requiring that these elements be balanced.

Proudhon and Bakunin reject Godwin's rational community for the same reason as they reject his rational individuality. A sharing of considered beliefs among intimate conversers is too narrow a form of mutual awareness for these later anarchists who seek community, like individuality, not only in the realm of intellect, but also in emotional and productive life. To achieve a wider and more varied consciousness, Proudhon and Bakunin envision anarchist society as composed of numerous productive enterprises, equal in power but diverse in kind, distinguished by their differentiated functions, related by negotiated bargains, and united by reciprocal dependence.[35]

A society organized as Proudhon and Bakunin wish would do something to create the multi-faceted individuality and community they use it to help reach. Being composed of enterprises which supply goods and services, it would foster awareness among its members of their concerns as producers, while developing their capacities for productive work.[36] It also would support rational individuality and community, to the extent that the productive activity it required encouraged the expression of independent thought. Only the emotional aspect of the individuality and community Proudhon and Bakunin seek would be unlikely, in their society, to be nourished much. Some shared emotional warmth could be expected from the team-work and cooperation occurring there, but feelings develop best in the intimate surroundings which Proudhon's and Bakunin's large, functionally differentiated society lacks.

The largeness and complexity of their good society also arrest growth of the rational and productive aspects of their envisioned community and self. Godwin had secured rational individuality and community partly by making society small and simple, so that its closely related members achieved mutual trust. Such trust, and the rationality it engenders, is harder to establish in Proudhon's or Bakunin's anarchy because its members, divided by their roles and ranks in complicated enterprises, and separated from participation in other enterprises by the rivalry that bargaining evokes, find it difficult to gain one another's confidence. Nor can productive consciousness and ability easily flourish in such enterprises, even though they are devoted to productive work. For the divided labor and managerial supervision they need for their success make activity in them so routine and servile that it does not foster productive power or awareness much.

Proudhon and Bakunin try to win support in their society for the rational and productive elements of community and self partly by the way they organize education. Both see education as an immunizer, which protects aspiring producers from the dividing and debilitating effects of work, through the methods of what Proudhon calls polytechnical apprenticeship. These methods consist first in 'having the neophyte producer carry out the entire series of industrial operations, moving from the simplest to the most difficult, however specialized', and second, in 'having him derive from these operations the principles that apply to each of them'.[37] Education thus organized serves individuality by making work more comprehensible. Since each producer who receives a polytechnical education learns the underlying theory of his work and knows from practical experience how his job relates to the rest, he sees the point of doing it, grasps its place in a larger whole and finds that far from sapping his rational and productive powers, it gives them added strength. His education also strengthens his involvement in productive and rational community by solidifying contacts with fellow workers. Producers who have taken turns performing others' work, and who share an understanding of its basic principles, are so closely attuned in attitude and outlook that they are not much separated by function or rank. Under anarchy, despite divided labor and managerial control, 'social communion [and] human solidarity are not vain words' because producers are held together 'by the memory of early struggles [and] the unity of their work'.[38]

The trouble with polytechnical education is its temporary benefits. Once completed, it no longer directly helps producers to relate as reciprocally conscious individuals. To extend its benefits to workers who have completed this initiation Proudhon and Bakunin propose to organize an anarchist economy so that producers in every industry, no matter how experienced, continue to work in turn at all the jobs their industry creates. Workers would also be encouraged to develop their skills and increase their knowledge by taking jobs in different industries. The only producers who would devote themselves to a single kind of work would be those who, on the basis of long experience, found that the positions they preferred to fill were fixed.[39]

The main difference between Proudhon's and Bakunin's way of developing community and self is in how they would organize the family. Bakunin seeks diverse and open families; Proudhon wants them to be uniform and enclosed. To give diversity and openness to children's family life Bakunin would weaken the hold of parents by forbidding the inheritance of wealth and would bring them under non-parental influence by charging society with their education.[40] Domestic openness and diversity would be provided for adults partly by leaving sexual unions untrammelled, 'neither violence, nor passion, nor rights previously surrendered' justifying regulation, and partly by making the care of children by their parents optional.[41]

The family Proudhon favors is more enclosed than Bakunin's, being organized as a permanent, monogamous household, in which inheritance is allowed. Its dominant figure is the father, who directs the lives of his children and his wife. The mother, 'fatally subordinate' to her husband, is charged with child-care and housework. Children, as the household's passive members, owe 'familial piety' and unqualified obedience to both parents.[42]

Bakunin's envisioned family is less of a remedy than Proudhon's for the inadequacies of their productive scheme as a support for community and self. These inadequacies, already noted, include a grave inability to nourish the emotional aspect of communal individuality and a substantial weakness, only in part corrected by polytechnical education and variety of work, as a source of the mutual trust needed to promote communal individuality in the rational and productive realms of life. Bakunin's family is unsuited for removing these inadequacies because it offers nothing more than do his economic and educational plans to overcome them. Encouraging the same mobility, diversity and rivalry in the domestic sphere as it encourages in productive life, his family, resembling an industrial enterprise, is no richer in warmth or trust.

Proudhon's family is better at providing warmth and confidence because its members, holding fixed positions in a hierarchy, are less troubled by the uncertainties that Bakunin's varied, egalitarian domestic life provokes. Emotional awareness and reciprocal trust are further strengthened in Proudhon's family by ties of devotion and love. The father certainly controls his wife and children, but to sustain and protect them, whether he profits thereby or not.[43] The mother shows her familial devotion by caring for the household and giving emotional support. She, no more than the father, considers the merits or achievements of needy relatives in deciding how to be of help. This 'sister of charity' gives her husband and children more than they deserve. 'Defeated or condemned, it is at her breast that [they] find consolation and forgiveness.'[44] It is thus the ascriptive character of domestic roles and the confidence and devotion it can be expected to evoke that make Proudhon's family more suitable than Bakunin's for developing the emotional and rational aspects of community and self. Producers in both theorists' anarchy are stymied to about the same extent in their search for self-development and mutual awareness. But while Bakunin's producers have nowhere to turn for their missing individuality and community, Proudhon's can turn to their families. There, in a stable, loving atmosphere, quite different from the volatile complexity of productive life, they find some, at least, of their needed trust and warmth.[45]

53

The educational and industrial organization that Proudhon and Bakunin back, even fortified by Proudhon's way of organizing families, gives insufficient help to individuals and community, as both anarchists admit. For producers remain at least somewhat estranged and stunted by supervised, divided work and separated by the conflict that bargaining among enterprises excites. To rid anarchy for good of these nagging defects, Proudhon and Bakunin suggest connecting its members with bonds of respect.

To respect another, for both writers, is to cherish him for what he, as an individual, is – an emotional, productive creature, responsible for his acts because able to choose them according to reasons. Thus conceived, respect has attitudinal and practical requirements. As an attitude, it enjoins care for the other person's sentiments and choices, empathizing with them, accepting them as one's own. As a practice, it calls for helping the other develop his thoughts and feelings, make his decisions and perform his chosen acts.[46]

Respect so understood provides the mediation between self-development and mutual awareness that Proudhon and Bakunin need, for by requiring care and nurture for what others think, feel and make, it supports the rational, emotional and productive elements in communal individuality. Mention of some ways Proudhon and Bakunin think respect gives this support will help clarify how it serves them as a mediator.

Two threats to communal individuality which respect easily defeats are force and fraud. When I coerce another or tell him lies, I weaken his identity and his consciousness of others as having rational, emotional and creative capabilities by manipulating or ignoring his power to think, feel or produce.[47] Since respect requires care for attributes of individuality that force and fraud negate, these cannot occur among its practitioners. The only way to affect another that accords him full respect is, after considering his plans and sentiments from his point of view, to offer arguments and evidence which convince him they are wrong. Such treatment is unqualifiedly respectful, because, while recognizing the capacities of those it affects to think, feel and make as *they* see fit, it helps them, within the limits of this recognition, to give these capacities added strength.

Proudhon and Bakunin can be criticized for proposing to mediate between individuality and community with respect, for though respect is a more effective mediator than Godwinian sincerity, and though its value as a social trait is less open to doubt, it is no less difficult to achieve. Even in Proudhon's or Bakunin's anarchy, producers would be baffled in trying to respect each other, because respect's requirements often are ambivalent. To respect another, I must help him perform his chosen act. But what if his act is one which, because it harms rational, emotional, or creative capabilities, is disrespectful? Respect urges me to reason with him, hoping to change his mind, but if my arguments are unavailing, however I treat him involves disrespect. For whether I help or hinder his attempt to carry out his action, I diminish the capabilities for which respect enjoins support.

To the charge that the sincerity he sought could not be achieved in full, Godwin had replied that since the individuality and community between which it had to mediate were limited, it could be incomplete. Proudhon and Bakunin cannot give such a reply to the charge that complete respect lies beyond reach, because their more complex individuality and community need mediation by a widely disseminated and fully applied respect. Since respect is both more needed and less attainable in Proudhon's or Bakunin's anarchy than sincerity is in Godwin's, theirs is harder to establish. But the point at issue here is unaffected by this drawback. Though Proudhon and Bakunin would have difficulty establishing anarchy with respect, respect is an appropriate mediator between the individuality and community they seek. Their anarchy is more complicated than Godwin's and harder to achieve, but like his its crux is a cohesive attitude which communally unites developed selves. Proudhon's and Bakunin's anarchy is thus fundamentally like Godwin's, because its organizing principle is the same.

KROPOTKIN: ANARCHY AS AN EXTENDED NEIGHBORHOOD

More than his predecessors, Kropotkin consciously extends the anarchist tradition, by scrutinizing and developing its earlier forms. One part of his revisionary effort is criticism of respect, both in its own right and as a mediator.

Respect had seemed a worthy attitude to Proudhon and Bakunin, because it fostered mutual consideration without what Proudhon called 'solidarité gênante'.[48] Respect puts an upper limit on the help that one must give. For I may go so far in helping you to think, choose or act that your dependence on me impairs your capabilities. Since respect is breached by excessive intervention, I must be careful not to give you too much help.[49]

While acknowledging the value of an attitude of respect, Kropotkin finds it too niggardly to serve as a mediating attitude for anarchy. 'Something grander, more lovely, more vigorous. . . must perpetually find a place in life.'[50] The fear of harming capabilities which a respectful person feels makes his intervention too inhibited. Anarchy requires outgoing relationships. It needs 'large natures, overflowing with tenderness, with intelligence, with good will, and using their feeling, their intellect, their active force in the service of the human race without asking anything in return'. In short, it needs benevolence.[51]

Since Proudhon used benevolence to unite members of the family, one might suppose that Kropotkin, developing the anarchist tradition, extends domestic devotion to society at large. This belief is incorrect, because for Kropotkin and Proudhon benevolence is different. Benevolence for Proudhon is owed only to persons who, as members of a family, are social intimates. Kropotkin thinks it is owed to anyone in need, even complete strangers.[52] Kropotkin's benevolence is also more egalitarian and mutual. Whereas benevolence in Proudhon's family is owed by parents to children, who are not expected to be benevolent in turn, it is owed in Kropotkin's society by each to all. No hint of the 'charity which bears a character of inspiration from above' is found in the benevolence Kropotkin seeks.[53] His is marked by a generous reciprocity that makes us one with each other, sharing and equal. That is why he often calls it mutual aid.

Kropotkin chooses benevolence rather than respect as the mediating attitude of anarchy not just because he finds it generous, but because he thinks its generosity better fits it to nurture his kind of self. There is more to Kropotkin's individuality than reasoning, emotions and productive force. It also includes 'inventive spirit', 'the full. . .expansion of what is original' in man, 'an infinite variety of capacities, temperaments and individual energies'.[54] The search for this sort of creative individuality is a dangerous adventure, which respectful (or sincere) treatment gives me little help to face. But if the treatment I receive from others is inspired by benevolence, my chance to become a creative individual grows. I can then rely on others to help me when in need, just because I am their fellow and regardless of defeats. Knowing they will support me should I fail in my quest gives me courage to seek uniqueness and creativity in the face even of great risk. Guyeau, notes Kropotkin, had posed the ultimate problem of creative originality by his reminder that 'sometimes to flower is to die'.[55] Anarchist benevolence solves even this grave problem by making the risk of the creative quest acceptable. A cruel end may await the seeker of individuality, but he is prepared by Kropotkin's anarchy even for death. 'If he must die like the flower that blooms, never mind. The sap rises, if sap there be.'[56]

Community, like individuality, has distinctive traits for Kropotkin, which make achieving it through benevolence appropriate. Proudhon and Bakunin gave anarchist community an emotional dimension and widened it to include productive work. Kropotkin further enlarges the anarchist conception of community by bringing more activities and a new feeling within its scope.

Reciprocal awareness among members of Kropotkin's anarchy occurs at every phase of life, in consuming as well as producing economic goods, in non-economic activities such as 'study, enjoyment, amusements', and in 'the narrow circle of home and friends'.[57] It is thus more pervasive in his society than in his predecessors'. Reciprocal awareness for Kropotkin is also richer than for them, because it includes, besides the rational, emotional and productive consciousness they mention, the feeling of solidarity they deem suspect. Since the awareness that I know you have and that you know I experience often arises in Kropotkin's anarchy from a sense of 'what any being feels when it is made to suffer',[58] it includes the sympathy for others' plight that Proudhon and Bakunin mistrust and that the fragmented production they make the source of reciprocal emotion does little to promote.

It is easy to see why an attitude of benevolence is a source of reciprocal solidarity. A benevolent person gives overt sympathy to anyone he encounters who needs help. Hence each member of a society in which benevolence is practiced cares for the others, knows they care for him and knows they know he cares. Benevolence is also an appropriate supporting attitude for the pervasive community Kropotkin seeks. Unlike sincerity, which is limited in application to intimate contexts such as conversation, or respect, which for Proudhon and Bakunin mainly affects treatment in productive life, benevolence, with its bearing on all activities, helps make all of social life communal.

It is partly because Kropotkin's community is so rich and pervasive that his anarchy can be likened to an extended neighborhood. Relations in small neighborhoods are apt to be benevolent and solidaristic in just the way Kropotkin envisages for anarchy. What he can therefore be conceived as doing is extending the neighborly relations which arise in contiguous small groups to the context of society at large. This interpretation of Kropotkin's enterprise is confirmed by his view of anarchy's social structure. For, like his predecessors, he thinks communal individuality unreachable if based only on a mediating attitude, and tries to organize society so that it gives communal individuality structural support. The social arrangement, called an agro-industrial commune, that he relies on for this purpose combines elements of earlier schemes of anarchist organization with new features designed to overcome their shortcomings and which make social relations neighborly.

The agro-industrial commune provides the same comprehensive education and the same occupational mobility as Proudhon's and

Bakunin's anarchy, for Kropotkin agrees that by giving an industrial society these attributes self-development and mutual awareness can be markedly increased. Proudhon and Bakunin had judged their educational and occupational arrangements to be powerful, if insufficient, as a social basis for their communal individuality. Kropotkin, striving for a communal individuality more elusive, because at once more particular and more solidaristic, cannot rely as much on occupational mobility and education for its achievement.

To provide the greater warmth and trust that his neighborly communal individuality demands, Kropotkin returns to Godwin's use of intimacy. But whereas Godwin had conceived of intimacy as occurring within the 'small and friendly circles' of a simple anarchy, Kropotkin extends it to a society that is larger and more complex. The main way he does this is by requiring that all activities, but especially production, be carried out in small, internally unspecialized units. The more intimate relations in such units and their less differentiated roles make them superior as a basis for solidaristic trust to the large, impersonal and internally specialized units of which Proudhon's and Bakunin's anarchy is composed.

To encourage the individual uniqueness, which is the other distinctive aspect of his ideal, Kropotkin puts even more stress than his immediate predecessors had on social diversity. It is 'the highest development of voluntary association in all its aspects, in all possible degrees, for all imaginable aims; ever changing, ever modified associations which . . . constantly assume new forms' that enables the members of Kropotkin's anarchy to become singular.[59] For among the varied units in Kropotkin's good society, each finds those that help him to develop a unique self.

One must doubt that benevolence, even in the context of an extended neighborhood, could mediate acceptably between the particularistic individuals and the solidaristic community that are the crucial elements of Kropotkin's ideal. More than his predecessors', the goal of Kropotkin's anarchy is discordant. Conflict between his unique individuals and their embracing community is more intense, and less controllable, than the conflict between the individuals and community earlier anarchists conceive. How can Kropotkin's social order, however well contrived, keep his seekers of uniqueness, even though benevolent, from rending communal ties? How can it prevent these ties from stymieing the creative quest? So bold is Kropotkin in defining the anarchist project that he seems seriously to diminish its prospects for success.

The truth of this charge and its bearing on the merit of Kropotkin's anarchism are crucial evaluative questions which the concluding chapter of this book takes up. But whatever the verdict on Kropotkin's boldness in discordantly defining his ideal, it has clear significance for the theoretical unity of anarchism. Though Kropotkin's ideal is more strife-ridden than his predecessors' it is the same ideal of communal individuality. Its elements may clash more markedly and be harder to achieve together, but they cannot be achieved apart.

Kropotkin's way of realizing his aspirations is further evidence of anarchism's deep unity. Committed like his predecessors to self-development and mutual awareness, and believing in the interdependence of these goals, he too tries to reconcile them with a mediating attitude and encourages this attitude with structural support. That Kropotkin should try to realize his discordant ideal in so unpromising a way may seem surprising. But it testifies once again to the unity of anarchist thought. For if even Kropotkin chooses attitudinal mediation as the path to communal individuality, then not only this path's destination, but the path itself must be one of anarchism's distinctive traits.

4

THE ANARCHISTS AS CRITICS
OF ESTABLISHED INSTITUTIONS

It is as critics of established institutions that anarchists receive the most acclaim. Even commentators who condemn their vision of future society find in their attack on the present one a certain appeal. For no matter how misguided the anarchists may be as visionaries, they point to defects in the existing order which tend to be overlooked.[1]

While the depth and penetration of the anarchists' criticism have long been acknowledged, its coherence has remained in doubt. For if liberty is regarded as the goal they are seeking, their choice of what to criticize is bound to seem confused. Anarchists whose chief goal was liberty would subject everything that curtails it to unlimited attack. Yet they refrain from utterly condemning features of the existing system such as authority and punishment, which interfere with liberty, and even incorporate versions of these coercive institutions into their model of an ideal regime. The thesis which serves as the main theme of this study, ascribing communal individuality to anarchists as their ultimate goal, serves to dispel the impression of incoherence in their criticism by giving all of their objections to existing institutions a justified place. The nuances and qualifications in their attack on the established order, which otherwise seem aberrant, are revealed as enjoined by their chief value, once its true character is recognized. Seeing the anarchists as seekers of communal individuality brings out their theory's coherence not only as a plan for social reconstruction, but also as a work of criticism.

Although each of the anarchists whose thought we are examining criticizes aspects of the existing social system that the others spare, all four agree that institutions usually taken for granted as integral parts of modern society deserve to be attacked. Legal government is, of course, the institution they most categorically condemn. Their opposition to authority, punishment and social inequality, while more limited, is just as intense. They all also find fault with industrial technology, though here their condemnation is remarkably nuanced. It is by analyzing their objections to these five institutions that the structure of their social criticism can most easily be revealed, for the anarchists use similar arguments, similarly qualified, to denounce all objects of their collective wrath.

LAW, GOVERNMENT AND UNANIMOUS DIRECT DEMOCRACY

Since the anarchists' view of legal government was examined in detail when it was compared with their view of censure no more is needed here as an account of their objections than a brief sketch. This section is less concerned to describe these objections than to clarify how far they extend. What it seeks to establish is whether anarchists call for the abolition of legal government no matter what its type, or whether, as some have thought, there is one type they accept.

It is of course as a hindrance to self-development and mutual awareness that anarchists condemn legal government. The generality and permanence of its controls, the remoteness of its officials and its use of physical coercion as its method of enforcement combine, say anarchists, to engender a distrust, resentment and impersonality that stifle individuals and break communal ties. Yet Robert Paul Wolff has argued that anarchists must accept one type of legal government as consistent with their conception of a good society. This is unanimous direct democracy.[2]

In a unanimous direct democracy everyone deliberates and votes on legislative proposals, and only those approved by everyone have force of law. One main reason Wolff thinks anarchists must support this form of government is because it dispenses with

physical coercion. Since the subjects of other governments dis-
approve on occasion of following the law, they must sometimes
be forced physically to do what it directs. But whenever the
citizen of a unanimous direct democracy follows a law, he carries
out an action which he personally approves. The esteem of all
citizens for the laws they must obey makes sanctioning them with
physical force unnecessary.

Even if anarchists endorsed government, provided it did not
physically coerce, they still would reject unanimous direct democracy, because such a government, despite what Wolff says,
resorts on occasion to physical force. A person who turns against
enacted legislation is no less forced to comply with it by a unanimous direct democracy than by other governments. The fact that
he once voted for a law he now opposes and that he can repeal it
when it comes up for review does not exempt him from coercion
for the period, however short, while it remains in effect. Nor are
persons unable to get their legislative proposals enacted exempt
from coercion, since they are forced by their government to do
without the laws they want.

But let us suppose that a unanimous direct democracy *can*
dispense with physical force. Even then it can have no place in a
complete anarchy, for it has other features besides physical
coercion that anarchists contest.

One is the deliberation through which the citizens of a unanimous direct democracy decide what laws to enact. It may seem
surprising that the anarchists, who so prize personal deliberation,
should oppose the collective deliberations of a unanimous direct
democracy. They reach this conclusion by condemning the special
kind of deliberation that occurs under such a government as
lacking in rationality and hence in worth.

In a unanimous direct democracy all citizens deliberate as
equals in the legislative assembly. Anarchists argue that the great
size of an assembly in which everyone participates inhibits forthright communication, invites rhetorical pandering, and relieves
citizens of personal responsibility for their decisions, all of which
prevent the independent scrutiny of arguments and evidence on
which rational deliberation rests. As Godwin complains, 'A

fallacious uniformity of opinion is produced, which no man espouses from conviction, but which carries all men along with a resistless tide.'[3]

Membership in a unanimous direct democracy could of course be limited so that the rationality of deliberation in the legislative assembly was not impaired by excessive size. But anarchists contend that deliberation, even in a unanimous direct democracy that is very small, remains pernicious. The fact that deliberation among legislators cannot always continue until a consensus is reached, but must often terminate with a vote, is enough to rob it of rationality. Where voting is used to end deliberation, says Godwin, 'the orator no longer enquires after permanent conviction, but transitory effect. He seeks rather to take advantage of our prejudices than to enlighten our judgment. That which might otherwise have been a scene of patient and beneficent enquiry, is changed into wrangling, tumult and precipitation.'[4]

Requiring the vote which enacts legislation to be unanimous further diminishes deliberative rationality by discouraging dissent. Godwin points out that where, to use Proudhon's words, 'the assembly deliberates and votes like a single man', 'the happy varieties of sentiment, which so eminently contribute to intellectual acuteness, are lost'.[5] The deliberating citizens, sensing the need to legislate, tend much more than in a majoritarian democracy to vote for whatever proposal seems most apt to win.

Nor must it be forgotten that the point of deliberation in a unanimous direct democracy is to legislate. Hence unanimous direct democracy suffers from the same defects, except perhaps physical coercion, as anarchists find in law. To anarchists, the equality of participation in a unanimous direct democracy is only dangerous, for it cannot rid the law which the assembly enacts of permanence, or generality. And it poses a danger of its own. As legislators, the assembled citizens must view proposals disinterestedly, from the impartial standpoint of the social whole. They must, in Godwin's words, 'sink the personal existence of individuals in the existence of the community [and] make little account of the particular men of whom the society consists'.[6] An assembly composed of citizens as anonymous as these is certainly not an *individualized* community. Its members may be bound together, but not so as to advance their self-development. And it easily degenerates into what Bakunin calls 'a sacrificer of living men,...where the real wills of individuals are annulled in that abstraction called the public will'. The diffusion in any democracy, but especially in a unanimous direct one, of a homogenizing spirit 'restrains, mutilates and kills the humanity of its subjects so that in ceasing to be men they become nothing more than citizens'.[7]

There is one main objection to the conclusion to which this analysis points, that anarchists would abolish legal government of every type. Some anarchists support the use of legal government where the conditions are lacking for anarchism's success. In such situations, they argue, legal government may be a necessary safeguard for domestic peace. Moreover, if it takes the form of a decentralized participative democracy, it may even advance the cause of anarchy through its educational effects. But the support of anarchists for legal government in adverse situations does not impugn the conclusion being defended here, which states only that in a mature anarchy legal government has no place. Since even unanimous direct democracy, which is the one form of government that anarchists might conceivably accept, receives their harsh strictures as repugnant to their ultimate ideal, they must certainly be regarded, despite the provisional support they give to legal government, as denying it any place whatever in an anarchist society that is complete.

AUTHORITY

Anarchists are often thought to hold that in their good society no one ought to exercise authority.[8] On this view, their opposition to authority is just as categorical as their opposition to the state. It is not only legal authority that receives their condemnation: they would abolish authority of *every* sort. There are statements by the anarchists that make them sound like authority's unrelenting foes, but the textual evidence is ambiguous enough to justify giving their attitude a close look. Do anarchists reject authority altogether, or are there some types they support? If they do support some, on what ground does their backing rest?

Authority can be exercised over belief as well as conduct, and in the private realm of groups and families, as well as in the public, social realm of life. Analysis of the anarchists as critics of authority must focus on their view of its application to public conduct. Concentrating on this narrow issue brings out what is distinctive in their attitude toward authority, which is anything but original so far as it applies to belief or private conduct.[9]

Authority, as applied to conduct, is a way to secure compliance with a directive, distinguished by the ground on which the directive is obeyed. You exercise authority over my conduct if you issue me a directive, and I follow it because I believe that something about you, not the directive, makes compliance the proper course. This something about you that elicits my compliance is something I attribute either to your *position* or to your *person*. I may submit to your authority because I think your position (say as president) makes you an appropriate issuer of directives, or because I think you are personally equipped (perhaps by advanced training) to direct my acts with special competence.[10]

Although anarchists accept personal qualities as sometimes entitling an issuer of directives to authority over private conduct, they deny that it ever entitles him to authority over conduct in the public sphere. We all lack the competence to do many private things and may be entitled in such cases to follow the direction of experts.[11] But since public conduct lies 'equally within the province of every human understanding', the personal qualities of those who direct it give them no right to be obeyed. In acting publicly, 'I am a deserter from the requisitions of duty, if I do not assiduously exert my faculties, or if I be found to act contrary to the conclusions they dictate, from deference to the opinions of another.'[12]

Though anarchists spurn personal qualities as a warrant for public authority, this does not mean that they would abolish public authority altogether. For they hold that under anarchy one still should sometimes obey issuers of directives that apply to public life out of regard for their position. The claim that they believe this faces several objections, which need to be rebutted before it can be effectively sustained.

What need to be considered first are statements by the anarchists which mock claims to public authority conferred by position. The clearest such statement is Godwin's, where he asks why one should obey another 'because he happens to be born to certain privileges; or because a concurrence of circumstances. . . has procured for him a share in the legislative or executive government of our country? Let him content himself with the obedience that is the result of force.'[13] Though this statement certainly condemns authority conferred by inherited or governmental position, it gives no basis for condemning positional authority altogether. That anarchists endorse authority in a state of anarchy, where its position can have different attributes, remains possible.

More troublesome as evidence against calling the anarchists supporters of positional authority is their repeated denunciation of authority in general. They must of course rule out authority conferred by position if they rule out authority of every type. This objection can be best allayed by noting that the anarchists' use of the term 'authority' is ambiguous. They often use it in the way described above, to designate a way to secure obedience based on an obeyer's belief about the one he obeys. But they also use 'authority' in a different sense to mean obedience procured by the rightful threat or use of physical force. To say that when they denounce authority they are *always* using it in the latter sense might seem reckless, but this contention is well supported by the texts.[14] Since what anarchists are denouncing when they attack authority is legitimate physical coercion, that they give positional authority a place in anarchy remains possible.

There is one more ground to doubt that anarchists embrace positional authority – its incompatibility with action based on reasoned argument. Action, to be commendable for anarchists, must rest on arguments and evidence that the deliberating agent judges for himself. 'The conviction of a man's individual understanding is the only legitimate principle imposing on him the duty of adopting any species of conduct.'[15] Though anarchists do not systematically ask how authority affects the rational basis of action, this effect is easy to describe.

Whenever an authority issues a directive to a subject who concludes from his own assessment of arguments and evidence that the act the authority prescribes for him is wrong, the authority prevents him from following his conclusion. For a subject cannot obey an authority and also follow his own conclusion, when the courses prescribed by the authority and his conclusion conflict. Since all authority sometimes keeps its subjects from following their rationally based conclusions about the merit of the action it prescribes, and since anarchists think the basis of one's action should be one's own rational assessment of its merits, it would seem that they must exclude positional authority, as much as personal, from regulating public conduct under anarchy.

The weak point in this argument is its assumption that for anarchists the value of reasoned argument is always overriding. If anarchists believed this, then they would indeed lack any normative basis in their theory to justify authority. But they do not believe it. As earlier chapters of this study show, the value of reasoned argument, while great for anarchists, is less than ultimate. It is a means to, and a part of, communal individuality, but is not itself supreme. Hence the fact that authority sometimes prevents action from resting on reasons leaves open the issue whether it has a place in anarchy. To resolve that issue the relations among authority, communal individuality and reasoned argument must be explored.

In deciding on the scope of reasoned argument, the anarchists are guided by their commitment to communal individuality. They support reasoned argument so far as they think it serves communal individuality, and they reject it so far as they think it causes communal individuality harm. The most obvious way reasoned argument harms communal individuality is by endangering social peace, as when it proves unable to ward off physical conflict. We have seen already that anarchists admit the frailty of reason and in cases of danger endorse controlling misbehavior with rebuke. What must now be added is that rebuke in a state of anarchy is a last resort. Against the insufficiency of reason and internalization to control misbehavior, authority is the anarchists' first defense; rebuke plays the role of a back-up, only to be inflicted when obedience to authority fails. Thus Proudhon and Bakunin call on 'opinion' and 'public spirit', not only to control misbehavior directly, but as means to enforce authority's decrees.[16] Godwin is more specific about how authority forestalls rebuke. When reason fails in a state of anarchy, most participants 'readily yield to the expostulations of authority'. But sometimes an authority's title to obedience is challenged. If the challengers disobey the authority, then and only then are they rebuked. 'Uneasy under the unequivocal disapprobation and observant eye of public judgment', they are 'inevitably obliged. . .either to reform or to emigrate.'[17]

The anarchists use authority, rather than rebuke, as the first defense against dangerous misconduct in order to protect communal individuality. Since rebuke, as the most coercive of censure's three aspects, can cause communal individuality much damage, it is important to anarchists that its use be minimized. If it was the first defense against misconduct, it would have to be invoked whenever reasoned argument or internalization proved ineffective. But as a back-up to authority, it need be invoked only on the few occasions when authority fails. As for the harm caused to communal individuality by authority, anarchists argue that if the authority is positional and properly restrained, this harm is slight.

Requiring authority to be positional rather than personal diminishes the harm it causes communal individuality by giving rational deliberation a wider scope. When I obey a personal authority, I refrain from evaluating the merit of the action he prescribes. Believing that some personal quality, such as special knowledge or insight, gives him the competence I lack to direct my conduct, I obey him without inquiring whether what he bids me to do is right. This inquiry is allowed by positional authority; for my obedience to such an authority does not depend on my assuming the correctness of his prescribed act. Since I believe that I ought to obey him because he occupies an entitling position, whatever the merit of his directives, I am free to assess them fully, so long as I follow them if my verdict is adverse. It is obvious, from this comparison, that positional authority allows rational deliberation more scope than personal authority does. And since rational deliberation is an intimate part of the anarchist ideal of communal individuality, it is also obvious that by requiring authority to be conferred by position the anarchists give their ideal significant support.

Even though positional authority does less damage to communal individuality than personal authority does, it still does damage. For even it requires subjects to do what they judge wrong. To alleviate the threat to their ideal that even positional authority presents, anarchists place restraints on it, designed so that it interferes as little with deliberation as is consistent with the need to maintain domestic peace. The restraints anarchists suggest for doing this specify who may fill positions of authority and how authority must be exercised.

It is usually by holding a specially designated office that one gains title to positional authority. Anarchists oppose giving authority to holders of special office. Thus Proudhon would 'eliminate the last shadow of authority from judges', and Bakunin rejects 'all privileged, licensed, official authority'. Rather than being confined to holders of designated offices, authority in an anarchy is, in Godwin's words, 'exercised by every individual over the actions of another'. All members of society must have a right to wield authority before its directives can deserve to be obeyed.[18]

To defend the legitimacy of authority exercised by all, anarchists rely on the comparison with legal government which they also use to defend censure. Wielders of authority who hold designated positions are like government officials in being too few to know the details of their subjects' situations. Hence they must treat them as an undifferentiated group. Such treatment must often seem mistaken to the subjects, who, more familiar with their situations, are apt to conclude that circumstances unknown to the authorities make it wrong to act as they direct. But if everybody has authority, it can obstruct deliberation less because then its wielders, being the same people as its subjects, but in different roles, can have more intimate knowledge of particulars. Equipped with this knowledge, they can bring their directives and the deliberations of their subjects into closer accord.

Besides requiring that authority in a state of anarchy be shared by everyone, anarchists also insist that its directives be concrete, not bound by or embodied in general rules, but flexible and specific.[19] Their argument for concrete authority borrows again from their comparison between censure and legal government. Authority which issues general directives, like government which issues general laws, impedes deliberation, even if its wielders are very numerous, because general directives, applying to broad classes of action, and hence unable to adjust much to specific circumstances, are often opposed by subjects for failing to take these circumstances into account. An authority whose directives are particular, being more able to consider individual situations, can better avoid contradicting the deliberations of its subjects about the merit of its prescribed acts.

Two conclusions are unmistakable from the analysis in this section. It is clear, for one thing, that, contrary to prevalent opinion and to what may be their own denials, anarchists give public authority a place in their good society. The authority they favor is extraordinarily limited, to be sure, but it is still authority, for it is a way to control behavior based on the subject's belief that something about the issuer of a directive gives him a right to be obeyed. The other noteworthy conclusion emerging from this analysis is that the anarchists' commitment to communal individuality easily explains both why they denounce most forms of authority and why they endorse their own distinctive type. Aware that authority obstructs rational deliberation, they fear it as a threat to their ideal. Unwilling to rely on reasoned argument alone as a behavioral control, they refuse to dispense with authority altogether. It is as an attempt to resolve the dilemma posed by these considerations that anarchists endorse the limited authority this section has described.

PUNISHMENT

If one uses nothing but the anarchists' explicit judgments as evidence of their attitude toward punishment, one must conclude that they condemn it unequivocally, for they denounce it with extraordinary force. Godwin, for instance, proclaims that 'punishment can at no time. . .make part of any political system that is built on the principles of reason', and Proudhon calls for the 'complete abolition of the supposed right to punish, which is nothing but the emphatic violation of an individual's dignity'.[20] This section argues for counting anarchists as punishment's supporters, despite statements like the foregoing in which they sound like unrelenting foes. Anarchists harshly oppose most forms of punishment, but they give a place in anarchy to one special kind. Their attacks on punishment are misread if taken as signs of utter condemnation.

There are three standard ways of justifying punishment: as retribution for the offender, as a means of reform by weakening his desire to misbehave, or, through the fear evoked by his suffering, to deter him from repeating, and others from committing, crimes. Godwin, who may here be taken as spokesman for all anarchists, opposes each of these justifications of punishment for warranting too many bad effects. Retribution is easily disposed of in this way since it fails to consider effects at all. Punishment is justified by retributivists because it is deserved, regardless of its consequences, which thus may cause considerable harm. Arguments for deterrence and reform, being based on consequences, need more elaborate rebuttal. Godwin weighs the likely effects of punishing for these reasons and finds that on balance they are bad.

It is the physical coercion imposed by punishment that Godwin sees as the source of its worst effects. Being coercive, punishment arouses fear in those it threatens. They are apt to do as they are told because they dread the suffering that might result from disobedience, rather than because they think what they are told to do is right. Obeying for this reason seems disastrous to Godwin, as to all anarchists, for whom the basis of self-development and communal solidarity lies in independent thought. 'Coercion first annihilates the understanding of the subject on which it is exercised, and then of him who employs it. Dressed in the supine prerogatives of a master, he is excused from cultivating the faculties of a man.'[21]

No matter how severe the bad effects of punishment may be, they cannot by themselves defeat the case for reform and deterrence, which claims that the bad effects are outweighed by the good. Thus Godwin must show not only that punishment is costly, but that its reformative and deterrent benefits are less valuable or less certain than they seem. The main benefit of reformative punishment is to weaken the desire to misbehave by evoking contrition and remorse. Godwin argues that the coercion punishment imposes prevents it from achieving this result. It 'cannot convince, cannot conciliate, but on the contrary alienates the mind of him against whom it is employed'.[22] Far from weakening criminal inclinations, punishment strengthens them, by making its victims resentful, not contrite. Reformative punishment thus fails to achieve its intended benefit because those subject to it become more anti-social than they were before. A similar argument is applied by Godwin to deterrent punishment, which is intended to reduce misconduct by overpowering criminal impulses with fear. Deterrent punishment can certainly make its victim more fearful of committing crime, but since it also arouses his hostility, it does not make him less likely to misbehave. Nor does the example of his punishment frighten others into eschewing crime. The spectacle of his suffering only makes them indignant, and more inclined to misbehave.[23]

By vigorously denouncing retribution, deterrence and reform, the anarchists certainly give the appearance of being utterly opposed to punishment. How can they support it, when they oppose the three main arguments deployed on its behalf? They do so by relying on a different argument, which justifies rebuke as punishment to prevent offenders from committing further crimes.[24] Even under anarchy there remains some danger of misconduct, which authority sanctioned by rebuke prevents. Though anarchists do not call this rebuke punishment, it is easy to show that they should.

Following common usage, anarchists conceive of punishment as a special type of suffering. For one thing, it must be imposed for a misdeed. The putting to death of a man 'infected with a pestilential disease' does not fall 'within the import of the word punishment' because the victim of such treatment has done no wrong.[25] Furthermore, the suffering called punishment must be imposed by an authority. That is why anarchists refuse to count as punishment acts of vengeance or of force applied in self-defense.[26] Though no anarchist gives punishment an explicit definition, the evidence just presented shows how for them it is implicitly defined. Anarchists, like most thoughtful writers on penal matters, define punishment as suffering imposed by an authority on an offender for his offense.

This definition gives the basis to establish that anarchists must classify the rebuke which occurs in their good society as punishment. Authorities in a state of anarchy are certainly the only persons who impose rebuke; for since, as the previous section indicated, no one in an anarchy lacks authority, any member who imposes rebuke must have it. It is equally obvious that under anarchy rebuke falls only on offenders for their offenses, because an anarchist authority may only rebuke a disobedient subject for a wrong *he* has done. Since the rebuke anarchists favor has the characteristics they quite sensibly identify as punishment's defining traits, calling it punishment seems a judgment they are forced to make.

They give two main arguments for refusing to make this judgment. Godwin refuses to make it by claiming that because rebuke controls without resort to 'whips and chains', it lacks the defining characteristic of punishment which consists in causing suffering.[27] The flaw in this argument is its assumption that the only kind of suffering is physical. Since the suffering rebuke causes, though purely mental, still is suffering, the anarchists, by justifying it, are justifying punishment.

Proudhon argues for denying that rebuke is punishment by claiming that under anarchy an obdurate offender, the only type who deserves rebuke, is not a human, but an animal: 'He has fallen to the level of a brute with a human face.'[28] No punishment befalls such an offender, no matter how severe his rebuke, because he is an animal, and animals, unlike humans, cannot be punished. This argument would work if Proudhon called obdurate offenders animals on the ground that their criminal behavior was involuntary. For punishment applies only to persons who can choose to stop committing crimes. But Proudhon believes that the obdurate criminal acts voluntarily. This 'ferocious soul' has 'placed himself outside the law' and can obey it if he tries.[29] His animality arises not from irresponsibility but from viciousness. By tracing his animality to this source, Proudhon removes the ground for denying he is punished when rebuked. For while it *is* impossible to punish offenders whose involuntary behavior makes them animals, there is no logical bar to punishing offenders whose animality comes from being vicious. The suffering rebuke causes such offenders, being imposed on them by an authority for their voluntarily committed crimes, must be accounted punishment by anarchists.

It becomes easy to understand how anarchists justify punishment once one sees that they are backing it when they advocate rebuke. The punishment anarchists favor is distinguished from all others by both its method and its aim; and it is on proof that what distinguishes it from other sorts makes it superior that their justification rests. Anarchist punishment is distinctive in method because it works entirely through rebuke and not at all through physical force. This gives it the advantages, described in prior chapters, that anarchists find in rebuke, of which the most crucial in the present context are its comparative mildness and its lesser tendency to illicit resentment. Anarchist punishment is distinctive in aim because it is imposed for none of the three standard reasons, but only to prevent offenders from repeating their crimes. Imposing it for this purpose avoids much cruelty justified by the standard aims. Retribution calls for punishment, even if it will do harm. Deterrence requires savagery, if it will frighten its victim or other possible offenders into refraining from crime. Deterrence and reform both warrant causing the innocent to suffer, either as an example or as therapy. The freedom of prevention from these shortcomings makes it markedly less offensive as the aim of punishment.

The anarchists resort to punishment of a limited kind, despite serious misgivings, in an attempt to resolve a dilemma much like the one that leads them to endorse a limited authority. Unwilling to rely on authority as a last resort to prevent misconduct, even under anarchy, where criminal inclinations would, in Godwin's words, 'be almost unknown', they insist on giving authority a penal sanction.[30] Fearful of the threat posed by this sanction to the integrity of their ideal, they hem it in with limitations designed to make its interference with communal individuality minimal. Thus punishment, like authority, far from being at odds with anarchy, is one of its integral parts.

SOCIAL INEQUALITY

Though anarchists are sometimes called radical egalitarians, against all differences of treatment, this view of them is even less persuasive than the view that they utterly reject authority and punishment.[31] Anarchist responses to the scourge of inequality are various, ranging from Godwin's plea for little more than equal opportunity to Kropotkin's scheme to redistribute advantages according to basic need. But since even Kropotkin's egalitarianism allows differences in benefits, it, no less than the others, is less than radical. This section makes sense of anarchist views on inequality of wealth and prestige by showing how their similarities and differences derive from a shared ideal. The anarchists' commitment to communal individuality confines their attacks on inequality to a limited range; differences in this commitment, along with special circumstances, explain why, within this range, each of their attacks has a separate place.

Godwin's objections to social and economic inequality are so emphatic, that if one considered nothing else, one might think his egalitarianism radical. He regards the evils of legal government as 'imbecil and impotent' compared to the evils of unequally distributed prestige and wealth.[32] The latter not only obstruct communal individuality, but are a main cause of legal government. For they so disrupt men's character and mutual relations that legal government must be imposed as a cohesive force. Social inequality for Godwin thus stands doubly condemned: both for impairing communal individuality by making it necessary to endure a state and for impairing communal individuality in its own right. It is by examining his account of the latter, direct impairment, that the main lines of his attack on inequality are easiest to grasp.

Predictably, he finds the harm done to character by economic inequality to lie in discouragement of rational independence. The poor, in an economically stratified society, even if they live comfortably, are burdened by a servility and by a compulsion to work, both of which 'benumb their understandings'.[33] The rich fare no better. Their rational capacities are sapped either by 'vanity and ostentation', by 'dissipation and indolence' or by 'restless ambition'.[34] Unequal prestige compounds the damage caused by unequal wealth. A society with ranks engenders deference and arrogance against which reason's counsel is unable to compete.[35]

Godwin also shows how inequality shatters the conversational relations which are for him the substance of community. 'The spirit of oppression, the spirit of servility, and the spirit of fraud', which are 'the immediate growth' of economic differences, are ample to disrupt men's unity as equals who honestly share their considered thoughts. The members of a society with economic differences too often harm their neighbors in order to get more wealth.[36] As for differences of rank, these, by making esteem depend on the prestige of one's position, create the same disruptive struggle in social interaction as differences of wealth create in economic life.

Besides opposing economic inequality for harming communal individuality, Godwin also condemns it as unjust. To allow differences of income or wealth, even without poverty, is to grant 'a patent for taking away from others the means of a happy and respectable existence'. It involves saying to the advantaged, 'you shall have the essence of a hundred times more food than you can eat and a hundred times more clothes than you can wear'.[37] Here we see a theme in Godwin that his successors stress more: benefits must be allocated in proportion to need.

Yet though Godwin denounces inequality with remarkable

77

vigor, he draws back from urging an equal distribution of prestige and wealth. 'The treatment to which men are entitled is to be measured by their merits.' 'The thing really to be desired is the removing as much as possible of arbitrary distinctions, and leaving to talents and virtue the field of exertion unimpaired.'[38] Far from backing radical equality, Godwin here urges that benefits be distributed unequally, according to desert. Hierarchy, he implies, is perfectly acceptable, so long as its advantages are earned. The only equality he here seems to support is the equal opportunity to excel.

The disparity between Godwin's attack on unequal treatment and his support for inequality proportionate to desert is explained by his beliefs about private property and distributive justice. He sees each of these as requiring an abatement of the radical egalitarianism that his attack on inequality would otherwise suggest.

Godwin believes that the rational individuality which equality helps produce is also much encouraged by private ownership. Rational individuals need a wide area of action in which to carry out their own decisions. The area of their discretionary action can be extended, and its boundaries secured, by making them property owners, conceived as allowed to use their holdings as they alone decide.[39] There is nothing in Godwin's commitment to private ownership that requires him to reject complete economic equality. Equal wealth can coexist with private property, if each individual has the same amount. But Godwin believes that wealth is in fact always unequally distributed where private property is held.[40] It is this empirical belief that prevents him from pursuing the egalitarian possibility that private ownership allows.

His conception of distributive justice also prevents him from pursuing it. Godwin's conception of distributive justice is a mixed one, which recognizes the claims of both productive contribution and basic need. The claim of need, we noted earlier, favors (though it does not mandate) radical egalitarianism by forbidding treatment that unequally meets the needs of life. Resources in a society governed by the claim of need are distributed unequally to be sure, but since the basic needs of individuals are similar, benefits to persons, in the form of need-satisfaction, are much the same.[41] The claim of contribution cuts against radical egalitarianism more sharply. Since the contributions of individuals vary more than their basic needs do, a society which rewards contribution not only allocates resources less equally than a society which rewards need, it also allocates personal benefits less equally. Thus Godwin's acceptance of productive contribution as a legitimate claim of justice helps – along with his beliefs about the effects on rational individuality of private ownership – to explain why his opposition to inequality is less radical than his denunciations make it seem.

The ambivalence of Godwin about the merit of equality is expressed in his view of its place in anarchy. He provides the equality that he thinks communal individuality and the claim of need demand by establishing a floor of basic goods. Each member of his anarchy, regardless of desert, receives a sufficient and equal supply of life's necessities.[42] The inequality that he thinks private ownership and the claim of contribution require is provided by the unequal distribution of luxuries and prestige. Once the claim of need is satisfied, the members of his anarchy receive economic benefits proportionate to 'the produce of [their] own industry', while esteem is meted out to them for 'the acquisition of talent, or the practice of virtue, or the cultivation of some species of ingenuity, or the display of some generous and expansive sentiment'.[43]

Godwin's successors are torn by the same conflicting considerations in their criticism of inequality. But, committed to more solidaristic conceptions of communal individuality, ownership and distributive justice, and having designed more egalitarian institutions, they come closer to supporting radical equality.

The objections to unequal wealth and prestige as bars to communal individuality, which Godwin was the first anarchist to raise, are repeated by all three of his successors. Where they differ from him is in gradually ridding anarchism of its anti-egalitarian, meritocratic elements. Proudhon retains some considerable commitment to private ownership and the claim of contribution, but these commitments are effaced in Bakunin's work and gone almost entirely from Kropotkin's. Thus, whereas Bakunin had still backed private ownership of goods used for consumption, though not production, and had proposed as the principle of economic distribution payment according to the number of hours worked, Kropotkin would have both consumption and production goods owned by the public and wants income to be distributed almost purely according to the claim of need.

As one argument for rejecting the claim of contribution and accepting that of need Kropotkin cites the technical difficulty of measuring how much any specific individual contributes to the value of economic goods. He takes the example of a coal mine and asks who among those involved in its operation adds most to the value of the coal. The miner, the engineer, the owner and many others, including those who built the railroads and machines that serve the mine, all contribute something to its final product, but it is impossible to say how much. 'One thing remains, to put the *needs* above the *works*.'[44]

He uses a similar technical argument to undermine the claim to private ownership. The distinction between instruments of production and articles of consumption is impossible to draw. 'For the worker, a room, properly heated and lighted, is as much an instrument of production as the tool or the machine.' His food 'is just as much a part of production as the fuel burnt by the steam engine'. His clothes 'are as necessary to him as the hammer and the anvil'.[45] Hence property arrangements which make ownership of the means of production public, while leaving articles of consumption in private hands, cannot be established. Both kinds of property must be either publicly or privately owned. Faced with these alternatives, Kropotkin has no doubt which anarchists will select. Exclusively private ownership is too divisive; hence completely public ownership must be their choice.

Behind his technical objections to private ownership and to paying producers according to their contribution lies Kropotkin's more fundamental argument that these practices harm communal individuality. Even if particular contributions could be measured, even if private ownership of consumption but not production goods could be arranged, Kropotkin would still reject these practices as incompatible with the unique individuality and the solidaristic community it is his purpose to achieve. Both payment for contribution and private ownership encourage personal acquisition, the first by rewarding it, the second by assuring the acquirer exclusive use of whatever he obtains. These practices also encourage a book-keeping mentality, according to which one gives in order to get. Society becomes 'a commercial company based on debit and credit'.[46] Acquirers who insist on equivalent exchange are unlikely to develop into benevolent, emotionally sensitive individuals, united by empathetic ties. Only by 'producing and consuming without counting each individual's contribution' and by 'proclaiming the right of all to wealth – whatever share they may have taken in producing it', can the communal individuality Kropotkin seeks be reached.[47]

Why do his predecessors, most notably Godwin, disagree? Mainly because their conceptions of individuality and community are different. Their conceptions of individuality, being more rationalistic than Kropotkin's, are more congenial to the separateness engendered by private property and by contribution as the criterion for pay. An independent thinker needs more protection from others than does a singular, emotionally developed self, for whom others' acts are more apt to be encouragements than incursions. The concept of community shared by Kropotkin's predecessors, being less solidaristic than his, helps further to explain why they disagree with him on the merit of the contribution standard and private property. The earlier anarchists are suspicious of solidarity as a danger to self-development. For Kropotkin, however, solidarity is one of the self's parts. Hence the sympathetic ties that so frighten his predecessors, and which they use the contribution standard and private property to combat, are for him essential to community. Viewing solidarity in this light, Kropotkin can not only do without the contribution standard and private property but must consider them abhorrent.

Besides having a basis in theory for his more radical egalitarianism, Kropotkin also has one in projected practice. His plan for anarchy – the agro-industrial commune – differs from earlier plans by building all the activities that normally occur in a large, industrial society into numerous, diverse, but small and internally unspecialized units. In a society so organized, benefits can be more equally distributed than in one composed of the more internally specialized, larger and more uniform units envisaged by Proudhon or Bakunin.

Yet, though Kropotkin's criticism of inequality is more sweeping than that of other anarchists, not even his is radically egalitarian. Radical egalitarianism, it will be recalled, is the thesis that everyone should be treated alike. There are at least two reasons why Kropotkin must reject it. His commitment to need as the criterion of distribution, while favoring movement toward radical egalitarianism, prevents him from accepting it completely, because needs cannot be satisfied without treating people differently. To satisfy the need for health, for instance, one must give more medical attention to the sick than to the well. The other reason why Kropotkin must reject radical egalitarianism stems from his conception of communal individuality. His conception, even more than that of the other anarchists, emphasizes a particularity which cannot possibly be achieved by treating everyone alike. Rather, it calls for individualized treatment, aimed at bringing out what in each person is singular.

Since even Kropotkin is kept by the fundamental principle of anarchism from radically condemning inequality, there must be a more accurate way to characterize his opposition. Calling Kropotkin, or any anarchist, a radical egalitarian is profoundly misleading, because it obscures a distinction in anarchist theory that is of great importance. Treating everyone alike ends two kinds of inequality which anarchists appraise differently. It not only eliminates the inequalities of rank, which all of them deplore, but wipes out the diversity that they regard as indispensable. What gives anarchist criticism of social inequality its special interest is that it focuses on hierarchy, not difference.[48] Each anarchist attempts, within limits set by his preconceptions, to diminish inequalities of rank while increasing those of kind. The hazards of this project explain why anarchist criticism of inequality is somewhat tentative. Since a richly differentiated society cannot be entirely free of ranks, it is no wonder that anarchists, though among the harshest critics of hierarchy, are still forced to put up with some.

Technology, for the anarchists, consists of the organization and machinery that transformed the productive process in their time. As modern industry developed, they grew more aware of how it undermined the social and psychological prerequisites for communal individuality. But even Godwin, who wrote when the industrial revolution was just starting, saw the main ways it threatens the advent of anarchy.

He, no less than his successors, believed that the division of labor, which was adopted by modern industry at an early stage, disrupts the intimate, fluid relations on which communal individuality so largely rests. He was also alarmed by mechanization, which, following on the heels of divided labor, separated skilled from unskilled workers, made unskilled labor even more routine, and put further barriers between ever more fragmented kinds of skilled work. Industrial technology is also feared by anarchists as a cause of social hierarchy. Besides dividing producers by their occupations, it widens disparities of prestige and wealth. Proudhon's image of industrial society, which well captures its inequality, is accepted by all anarchists. Such a society is like 'a column of soldiers, who begin marching at the same time, to the regular beat of a drum, but who gradually lose the equal spacing between their ranks. They all advance, but the distance between the head and the foot of their column continuously grows; and it is a necessary effect of this movement that there are laggards and strays.'[49]

But what most concern anarchists about technology are its psychological effects. Both the occupational fragmentation and the inequality that industrial technology promotes are blamed by anarchists for causing insincerity, disrespect and malevolence, the exact opposites to anarchy's mediating attitudes. The exhausting monotony of so much industrial labor is also feared by anarchists as psychologically dangerous. Armies of unskilled workers, who spend long days at repetitious, enervating tasks, have a stunted sensibility that makes the growth of empathic attitudes difficult.

Besides fearing technology's social and psychological virulence, the later anarchists also dread its political effects. Proudhon's apprehension was that the managerial authorities the new technology was creating would use their expertise to dominate their subordinates in the workplace. Bakunin anticipated something more ominous: that as technology became more complicated and more difficult to understand, and as each industry grew more dependent for its efficiency on its relations with the rest, technical managers would gain such political ascendency that everyone would fall under their control. What threatened was nothing less than 'the reign of scientific intelligence, which is the most aristocratic, despotic, arrogant and contemptuous of all regimes. A new class, a new hierarchy of real and fraudulent experts will arise; and the world will be divided into a minority, dominating in the name of science, and a vast majority, reduced to ignorance.'[50]

One might expect that since industrial technology so frightens anarchists, they would condemn it absolutely and in their good society would give it the smallest possible place. But they are far from being Luddites. Rather than campaigning to destroy technology, they seek to harness it, so that as it develops, it gives to communal individuality increasing support. Their verdict on technology as compared to the other institutions they qualifiedly condemn is thus more positive. Whereas they resign themselves to some authority, punishment and hierarchy as necessary evils, they welcome industrial technology as an unruly but promising servant. It is only untrammelled technology that they deem virulent; appropriately controlled technology is for them a growing source of hope.

Each anarchist has a somewhat different plan for exploiting technology. The most instructive is Kropotkin's, because it uses his predecessors' main devices as well as new ones of his own design to harness the more complex technology of the late nineteenth century.

His starting point is Godwin's proposal to divide production between a subsistence sector, to which everyone devotes the same short period of time, and a luxury sector, to which they devote what time they like.[51] Godwin had claimed that this way of dividing production allows work to be completely mechanized without causing individuality or community harm. They cannot be harmed by work in the luxury sector, because it is satisfying and voluntary. Nor can they be harmed by work in the subsistence sector, which Godwin thought would take only a half hour to complete and which all would share equally. Kropotkin buttresses these claims of Godwin's by saying more about how the divided economy they both favor should be arranged.

Luxuries, for Kropotkin, are not only produced voluntarily, they are also for the most part produced by their consumers. A person wanting a luxury is not to be supplied with it by someone else, but is to join with others who desire it so that together they can produce it for themselves. This cooperative method of producing luxuries is seen by Kropotkin as fostering individuality by enabling each producer to acquire diverse tastes and skills, and as fostering community by enabling those who share these tastes and skills to cultivate them in concert.[52]

Since Kropotkin, with much actual experience of industrial production behind him, believes that subsistence work must take about five hours per day, rather than the half hour Godwin had expected, he cannot depend as much on its insignificance to prevent it from harming communal individuality. To overcome the threat to the anarchist ideal that five hours of daily routine labor pose, he relies partly on the comprehensive education and occupational mobility introduced into the anarchist tradition by Proudhon. He repeats Proudhon's reasons why these practices alleviate not only the psychological and social damage caused by industrial technology, but also its political damage. Managerial technicians in an anarchist economy, aware, because of comprehensive education, that everyone can do their job, and because of occupational mobility, that their job is temporary, have neither the ability nor the desire to use their positions as means of technological domination.

Besides citing his predecessors' arguments for comprehensive education and varied work, Kropotkin adds a new one, drawn from his assessment of productive trends. As technology develops, he says, the efficiency of monotonous, specialized labor declines. 'Humanity perceives that there is no advantage for the community in riveting a human being for all his life to a given spot, in a workshop or mine; no gain in depriving him of such work as would bring him into free intercourse with nature, make of him a conscious part of the grand whole, a partner in the highest enjoyments of science and art, of free work and creation.'[53] Educating producers comprehensively and giving them varied work have always served efficiency by encouraging technical innovation. Not even learned scientists can innovate more fruitfully than knowledgeable workers. Until recently, Kropotkin admits, the advantage for innovation of a broad education and unspecialized work was outweighed by the efficiency of specialized training and divided, routine work. But technical trends have finally tipped the balance in favor of more integrated production. Electric power, hand-held machine tools and mechanical farm implements are the most telling of the innovations he cites as enabling an advanced industrial economy to operate efficiently, though run by comprehensively educated producers, doing varied, unspecialized work.[54]

Kropotkin does more than show the growing practicality of the anarchist plan for harnessing technology: he adds provisions to make technology a still better servant. One is the organization of industry into small productive units, for the more intimate relations in small workplaces and the less specialized nature of their jobs make them superior as supports for self-development and mutual awareness to impersonal, monotonous production in large factories. Another new provision of Kropotkin's plan is the uniting of industry with agriculture. Bringing farm and factory together, so that producers can spend time in each, gives them a more varied choice of jobs than they would enjoy without mobility of occupations between the industrial and agricultural sectors.[55] The last of Kropotkin's new provisions is economic self-sufficiency. The members of his anarchy themselves produce the goods that they consume. He devotes great ingenuity to showing how contemporary technical developments make self-sufficiency easy to achieve. Yet its main advantage for him is not its practicality, but its wider choice of occupations. A self-sufficient economy, provided that, like anarchy's, it is a large one, offers more varied work than does a specialized economy, because its complement of industries is fuller.

It is tempting to conclude from the foregoing analysis that anarchists rely so much on technology as to warrant including them among its venerators. This conclusion overlooks the qualifications in their support. Nineteenth-century venerators of technology, whether Marxists or free-enterprisers, trusted in its untrammelled growth.[56] Anarchists, in contrast, counted on technology only if it was controlled stringently. By repudiating most organizational aspects of industrial technology, while exploiting its mechanical aspects, anarchists offered a vision of its future that in the nineteenth century was already engaging. In light of the disappointment with free technical development that is so widely felt today, the anarchist course between Luddite contempt and scientistic celebration has even more appeal. For how, except by limiting technology, while also working for its selective growth, can communal individuality in an industrial society possibly be increased?

THE COHERENCE OF ANARCHIST CRITICISM

This chapter has confirmed the longstanding appreciation of the anarchists as unusually severe critics of modern society. Their utter condemnation of government and law is endorsed by no one else. Nor have theorists gone further than the anarchists in subjecting authority, punishment and inequality to attack. But something else emerges from the analysis in this chapter besides reaffirmation of a well-known truth. By tracing the anarchists' social criticism to its source in their commitment to communal individuality, this analysis has put to rest the doubts about its coherence which are prompted by its failure to condemn categorically all restrictive institutions. The qualifications in favor of authority, punishment and inequality which anarchists introduce into their social criticism stand forth not as symptoms of confusion, but as faithful expressions of their thought. Had the anarchists failed to make these qualifications they would have been inconsistent, for had they given full vent to their critical impulses, by categorically denouncing everything they abhor, they would have disregarded the imperatives of their chief value. Their commitment to communal individuality thus not only explains why, to be consistent, anarchists qualify their social criticisms, but also accounts for why their criticism, while severe, is not extravagant. The goal of anarchism, being composed of norms whose merger is precarious, enjoins a social criticism that has nuance and balance.

5

ANARCHIST STRATEGY: THE DILEMMA OF MEANS AND ENDS

Efforts to ascribe a distinctive strategy to anarchists, though often made, cannot succeed, because their strategies are too diverse to have a common character. Claims that all anarchists are reckless terrorists, or saintly pacifists, or messianic 'primitive rebels' widely miss the mark.[1] These descriptions do fit some anarchists, at some stages of their careers, but as applied to anarchist strategy in general they are inaccurate. Even the most cautious and plausible description of anarchist strategy – as eschewing 'political action' – does not fit all cases, not even all of those under study here.[2] Proudhon put his trust in the thoroughly political Louis Napoleon. Bakunin, who relied, as a means to anarchy, on the elimination of inheritance, thought it might be legally abolished through 'a series of gradual changes, amicably agreed to by the workers and the bourgeoisie'.[3]

Impressed by the differences in anarchist strategy, some commentators, instead of ignoring them, make them the basis for classifying anarchism into types. 'In examining the basic forms of anarchism', writes Irving Horowitz, 'what is at stake is not so much alternative models of the good society as distinctive strategies for getting there.'[4] He goes on to distinguish eight types of anarchism, each supposedly marked off by strategic differences. The inadequacy of his classification is easy to see. Most of its types, such as utilitarian, peasant and collectivist anarchism, are marked off from the others not by their strategy but by their method, aspiration, or source of support. Only two of the types mentioned – conspiratorial and pacifist anarchism – are strategically distinct. It is possible to come closer than Horowitz to classifying anarchists by their strategies, but this project is no more likely to succeed than that of proving that their strategies are all basically the same. Anarchist strategy is too diverse to be called unified, but its diversities cannot be used to classify it because they are too unsystematic.

The thesis guiding this study of the anarchists, that communal individuality is their chief goal, provides a point of vantage from which the character of their strategy can be more accurately perceived. Seen from this vantage, the anarchists' strategy has no importance for the unity and classification of their thought. These are determined by the similarities and differences in their ideals of communal individuality. Strategy, as the means to these ideals, is subordinate to them and to empirical judgments about how, in the face of great adversity, they may most efficiently be reached. For the anarchists, therefore, strategy, being an attempt to achieve communal individuality in a hostile world, poses this grave dilemma: to find a path to communal individuality that eschews the fraud and physical coercion which, though effective means of social action, communal individuality forbids. The anarchists we are studying do not give this dilemma the same response. This chapter follows them in their unavailing search for a solution.

GODWIN: 'TRUSTING TO REASON ALONE'[5]

No anarchist is more resolved than Godwin to use reasoned argument among independent thinkers as the means to reach communal individuality. His commitment to intelligent, sincere conversation as the essence of a good society enjoins him to rely on argument, for unless the aspirants for his kind of anarchy become forthright and rational as they build it, the society they create, having unreasonable, dishonest members, will not be anarchic. Yet though Godwin sees that reasoned argument must be his strategy, he doubts whether, to reach his radical and fiercely resisted goal, it has sufficient strength. His work on strategy attempts to meet this doubt by showing the ineffectiveness as means to anarchy of non-rational tactics, and the power of rationality to direct history's course. But misgivings remain, which prompt him to endorse methods for reaching anarchy that are less than rational. Faced by the dilemma that all anarchists confront, even the scrupulous Godwin compromises his moral commitment for some hope of success.

The strategy Godwin most despises is the one most inimical to reason: the strategy of using physical force. Force inspires attitudes as detrimental to the process of attaining anarchy as to its maintenance. The imposers of force 'become obdurate, unrelenting and inhuman'. Its victims 'are filled with indignation and revenge'. 'Distrust is propagated from man to man, and the dearest ties of human society are dissolved.'[6] Using force as a means to anarchy only puts it further beyond reach.

Godwin also opposes strategies more compatible with reason than force of which the most significant is organization. Organization, he thinks, 'has a more powerful tendency than perhaps any other circumstance in human affairs, to render the mind quiescent'.[7] The members of an organization are strongly disposed to follow the opinions of their group. By doing so, they may serve their group's purpose, but they also lose their mental independence. This loss, while irrelevant for many purposes, is disastrous for that of reaching anarchy, since anarchy is a condition of utmost mental independence. Anarchists cannot organize, because organizing takes from their objective one of its essential traits.

In order to vindicate a strategy of reason, Godwin must do more than prove that as means to anarchy non-rational measures fail. He must show, against serious objections, that reasoned arguments are effective. Godwin believes that reasoned arguments are a sure means to anarchy, because of their great power to convince. So firmly can they convince people of anarchy's supreme worth that all will work unstintingly for its assured achievement. This belief faces metaethical, psychological and socio-political objections, to all of which Godwin has responses.

The weak point in Godwin's belief, so far as concerns metaethics, is its contention that evidence and reasons are logically sufficient to establish anarchy's supreme worth. Ascriptions of supreme worth, being ultimate evaluations, depend for their validity not only on undeniable evidence and reasons, but on contestable choices. Thus even if I accept the case for anarchy as being in agreement with facts and logic, I need not regard anarchy as of highest worth, for I may still consistently choose to set supreme value on something else.

To Godwin this objection has no weight, because in metaethics he is a cognitivist. Ultimate evaluations for him, far from involving choices, depend on nothing but facts. To establish values we examine the structure of the world and 'declare that which the nature of things has already decreed'.[8] There is no room from this metaethical perspective to doubt the possibility of rationally assured agreement on ultimate worth. Everyone can be convinced to accept the same value as supreme, because its identity depends solely on facts that everyone can know. As an account of how ultimate value is identified, Godwin's metaethic is too unqualifiedly cognitivist to be acceptable. But even if it were acceptable, this would do little to vindicate his strategy, whose heavy reliance on reason also faces non-metaethical objections.

Godwin's strategy is suspect psychologically for giving the motive of rational conviction decisive weight. Knowledge is not compelling: one need not do what one knows is right. To answer this objection, Godwin shows the weakness of non-rational motives. The fact that people successfully resist their sensual or short-sighted impulses shows how 'slight and inadequate' they are. That these impulses can be 'conquered or restrained. . .by the due exercise of understanding', is proved daily by experience.[9] Yet after doing his best to show the psychological force of reason, Godwin still doubts it can always prevail. An adverse piece of evidence that must be faced is that of people who fail to follow their convictions. To save his psychology from being dismissed as empirically unfounded, Godwin makes this claim: If I fail to do an action which I believe is right, my failure proves that my belief lacks a rational foundation. 'When the understanding clearly perceives rectitude, propriety and eligibility to belong to a certain conduct, . . .that conduct will infallibly be adopted.'[10] Hence what is shown by my failure to do something I believe right is not that my inclinations overpower my convictions, but either that my convictions do not enjoin the act, or else that they counsel against doing it.

This claim has the untenable implication that anyone who says he fails to follow his convictions mistakes their meaning or their source. Certainly, we sometimes make mistakes on these matters, but to say we always do is implausible. Some people have settled, systematically backed convictions, on which they usually act. It is more credible to believe such persons when they report failing to follow their convictions than to charge them with misunderstanding what their convictions say. And since belief in failure to follow rationally held convictions often is well founded, Godwin's claim that such convictions always determine conduct fails.

The final objection to Godwin's strategic use of reason points to his own analysis of how corrupt and hampering institutions 'poison our minds, before we can resist, or so much as suspect their malignity'. The 'disparity of ranks' in all existing societies inspires 'coldness, irresoluteness, timidity and caution'.[11] The impersonality and coerciveness of existing legal governments make subjects devious, servile and unthinking. How can Godwin choose reason as his strategy, when he sees it as obstructed by the very institutions it is supposed to overthrow?

He answers with an account of the growth of natural science. 'Hitherto it seems as if every instrument of menace or influence has been employed to counteract [science].' But it has made progress nonetheless. For the mind of man cannot 'choose false-hood and reject truth, when evidence is fairly presented'.[12] Since adversities have not kept reasoned argument from causing scientific progress, they cannot keep it from causing social progress either. 'Shall we become clear-sighted and penetrating in all other subjects, without increasing our penetration on the subject of man?'[13]

The analogy with natural science gives hope that for reaching anarchy reasoned argument will soon be effective, despite its past and continuing impotence. 'How imperfect were the lispings of . . .science, before it attained the precision of the present century?' 'Political knowledge is [now] in its infancy.' Hence its advances are bound to be slow. But since progress in natural science accelerated, as its growing number of findings became better established and more widely known, we can expect progress toward anarchy to be faster, as stronger reasons in its favor are adduced.[14] No matter that anarchy now has few partisans, whose arguments are usually dismissed; the early partisans of science met a similar fate. 'If the system of independence and equality be the truth, it may be expected hourly to gain converts. The more it is discussed, the more will it be understood, and its value cherished and felt.'[15]

So doubtful is Godwin of reaching anarchy through argument that he draws on his shaky analogy with science for evidence of more than reason's persuasive force. This analogy, he thinks, shows the obstacles to the growth of reason as being not impediments to anarchy, but preconditions, and even helps. Progress in natural science meets obstacles in the form of 'extravagant sallies of mind' which 'an uninformed and timid spectator' might think would lead to 'nothing but destruction'. 'But he would be disappointed.' These extravagances 'are the prelude of the highest wisdom...The dreams of Ptolemy were destined to precede the discoveries of Newton.'[16] Social progress meets analogous obstacles, the most serious being legal government and unequal wealth. The former, though utterly expunged from a mature anarchy, prepares for it by assuring the peaceful setting in which a still nascent reason can grow.[17] As for unequal wealth, it too, while no part of future anarchist society, is a needed preparation. 'It was the spectacle of inequality that first excited the grossness of barbarians to [the] persevering exertion' on which an advanced economy like that of anarchy rests.[18] The obstacles to anarchy thus need cause no dismay, for even the most serious are objective pre-conditions, which must develop before the arguments for anarchy can take effect.

To clinch his case for reason, which he properly sees cannot be vindicated by reference to the analogy with science alone, Godwin describes the process through which he expects arguments for anarchy to prevail. The thesis informing his account of this process is that the main determinant of practice is belief. 'Wherever the political opinions of a community, or any portion of a community, are changed, the institutions are affected also.'[19]

Guided by this thesis, Godwin aims to show that everyone can be convinced to work for anarchy through the force of arguments known at first only to very few.

What he envisages is that the few individuals who happen to be convinced anarchists will serve as 'guides and instructors' to everyone else.[20] Through the same 'candid and unreserved conversation' that is the organizing principle of an established anarchy, they will 'extensively communicate the truths with which they are acquainted'. These truths, being forthrightly transmitted in an intimate setting, will be so cogent to their hearers that they 'will be instigated to impart their acquisitions to still other hearers'. Thus the 'circle of instruction will perpetually increase'.[21]

Though Godwin relies on reasoned argument as the impetus for the first steps toward anarchy, he does not contend that everyone, or even a majority, must embrace anarchism before social reconstruction begins. Rational beliefs are certainly the main shapers of practice for Godwin, but he is not blind to the effects of practice on these beliefs. He would therefore accompany the later diffusion of anarchist convictions with a gradual, voluntary decentralization of power and equalization of ranks, designed to inspire belief in anarchy to spread further. National governments would first give way to a loose confederation of small 'parishes' governed by democratically elected 'juries'. At later stages these juries would lose first their right to punish physically and then their right to legislate. Finally, they would be 'laid aside as unnecessary'. Thus would convictions and practices advance reciprocally and by degrees to their final culmination: 'one of the most memorable stages of human improvement, . . .the dissolution of political government, of that brute engine, which has been the only perennial cause of the vices of mankind'.[22]

Because he gives such great responsibility for reaching anarchy to a few enlightened individuals, Godwin has been accused of 'elitist disdain'. 'Convinced of his superiority of intellect', he and his few partisans allegedly place themselves 'above the mediocre, the petty, the base, the dull and the deceived'.[23] This charge, which makes Godwin sound like a contemptuous manipulator of the masses, misrepresents his view of their intellectual capacities and of how their allegiance should be won. While Godwin does think most people lack rational, independent judgment, he also thinks that they will someday have it.[24] Ignorance and irrationality are temporary conditions, which reasoned argument, aided by the gradual reform of institutions, can overcome. Elitist manipulation is therefore no part of Godwin's strategy. His partisans are not to create an anarchist society behind the masses' backs, but are to start the process through which rational individuals choose anarchy as the regime *they* create. Godwin's anarchy, as he carefully points out, does not result from 'the over-earnest persuasion of a few enlightened thinkers, but is produced by the serious and deliberate conviction of the public at large'.[25]

Though Godwin does not compromise the rationality of his strategy with manipulative fraud, he does compromise it with force and organization. While believing fervently in the effectiveness of argument, he still acknowledges situations where it might fail. What of a crisis, such as a war or revolution, which turns the anarchists and their critics into hostile foes? To argue independently 'in the moment of convulsion' might be suicidal; the anarchists may have to organize 'something in the nature of association' in order to survive.[26] And what of a situation where the anarchists, now a vast majority, face a few incorrigible opponents? In this circumstance, says Godwin, they may use physical coercion, partly because a complete anarchy might otherwise never be established, but mainly because coercion will not actually have to be imposed. Since their 'adversaries will be too few and too feeble to be able to entertain a serious thought of resistance', they will be compelled to accept anarchy by the mere threat of force.[27]

By endorsing force and organization as strategies, albeit in unlikely situations, Godwin shows his failure to solve the dilemma of anarchist strategy by trusting to reason alone. It would be presumptuous, however, to conclude from his failure that the dilemma is insoluble. Perhaps anarchy could be reached without fraud or coercion through a different path than Godwinian reason. The attempts of his successors to solve the dilemma need to be examined as preparation for deciding if a solution can be found.

PROUDHON: WAITING FOR THE REVOLUTION

Because Proudhon's conception of communal individuality gives more stress to cooperative work and less to rational independence than Godwin's, it admits a wider range of strategies. Proudhon is able, without inconsistency, to endorse organization, and can in good conscience advocate forms of persuasion not purely rational. But though his conception of communal individuality gives him more strategic leeway than Godwin, he succeeds no better in solving their shared dilemma. His untainted strategies are no more effective than Godwin's reason; his effective ones are no purer than the physical coercion Godwin chose.

Proudhon does not think, any more than Godwin, that anarchy can be established at any time. Rather, he too believes, though for somewhat different reasons than Godwin, that government and inequality must first prepare the way for anarchy through their effects. Inequality serves to stimulate exertion. 'If the property owner had tired of appropriating, the proletarian would have tired of producing.'[28] Government engenders self-restraint. It was 'by means of its tribunals and armies', that government 'gave to the sense of right, so weak among the first men, the only sanctions intelligible to fierce characters'.[29] Only when government and inequality complete their preparatory work (a time which Proudhon thought had occurred just recently) can the search for a strategy to achieve anarchy profitably begin.

At the start of his career Proudhon was as committed as Godwin to a strategy of reasoned argument. He explicitly rejected not only coercive tactics, but imperfectly rational ones. 'Stimulate, warn, inform, instruct, but do not inculcate', he prescribed.[30] Inculcation had to be avoided not only because anarchist ideals forbade it, but because reasoned argument was certain to succeed. Once his principles had been disseminated, Proudhon then believed, they would surely be applied. 'Wherever this discourse is read or made known', he wrote in his first important book, 'there privilege and servitude will sooner or later disappear.'[31] But whereas Godwin espoused a strategy of reason for his entire life, Proudhon quickly saw its inadequacies. Readier to admit the strength of anarchy's opponents, less sanguine about the compelling force of rational conviction, and more doubtful, owing to intervening failures, of history's progressive course, he soon despaired of reasoned argument and began to seek an equally pure but more effective substitute.

His search led first to a scheme for free credit, a 'People's Bank', lending without interest to anyone who could put money to a productive use. Such a bank, Proudhon believed, would pave the way for anarchy by enabling producers who lacked capital to start their own enterprises. These enterprises, being independent of the established social order, would form an ever growing network of alternative institutions for the nascent anarchist society.

As a strategy for anarchists, the People's Bank has no advantage over reasoned argument. To be sure, it is as morally legitimate, because it makes no use of force or fraud. Only 'holders of government bonds, usurers, . . .and big property owners' would find the Bank unprofitable, and they would be too weak to stop its growth. As it developed, they would be convinced, 'by a sense of the inevitable and concern for their interests to voluntarily change the employment of their capital, unless they preferred to run the risk of consuming it unproductively and enduring swift and total ruin'.[32] It would thus be through their uncoerced and unmanipulated decisions that their resistance would be overcome.

Though free credit and reasoned argument are equally pure, they are also equally ineffective. The opposition to anarchy is much too strong to quell by the enticements of free credit. But even if Proudhon was right to think his Bank could sway all opponents, he would still have been wrong to expect it to achieve anarchy. The Bank, even with everyone's support, would still be a mere monetary device, no 'solvent of all authority' destined to 'shift the axis of civilization'.[33] It is because he expected such remarkable results from a rather trivial institution that Proudhon has rightly acquired the reputation of a money crank.

He did not remain committed to free credit for long. The failure, during the revolution of 1848, of his effort to operate a People's Bank prompted him to reassess his strategy. Impressed by the militance of his opponents, and appalled by the futility of the tactics he had just espoused, Proudhon turned to Louis Napoleon, the emerging dictator who, on 2 December 1851, had overthrown the Second Republic in a *coup d'état*. 'The Second of December is the signal for a forward march on the road to revolution', proclaimed Proudhon, and 'Louis Napoleon is its general.'[34] Though Bonaparte was no anarchist, anarchists must work with him, because his plans for social renovation, whatever their intended purpose, would have the effect of bringing anarchy closer.

It is hard to imagine a strategy more repugnant to anarchist principles than collaboration with Bonaparte. Even if Bonaparte had been a scrupulous official, Proudhon should have abhorred him. But he was corrupt and arbitrary, a wielder of naked force. Nor can Proudhon's collaborationism be pardoned as effective, since Bonaparte, whose leftist sympathies were nominal, did not and could not have been expected to advance the cause of anarchy. Collaboration with Bonaparte, being both forbidden by anarchist ideals and useless for realizing them, was for Proudhon the worst possible tactic.

Having found the paths of reason, free credit and collaboration to be dead ends, Proudhon for a while gave up the search for a legitimate, effective strategy. Consoling himself with confidence that history in the long run was on his side, he took up a stance of what he aptly called 'attente révolutionnaire'.[35] There was no way for anarchists to make the 'ignorant, impulsive majority. . . recognize the truth, sense its depth, its necessity, its supremacy, and freely accept it'. Yet anarchy would still some day be achieved. 'The conversion of societies is never sudden. . .It is assured, but one must know how to wait for it.'[36] Waiting did not mean complete passivity; Proudhon worked hard on 'serious long-term studies addressed to the future and another generation'.[37] But for about ten years he set the dilemma of anarchist strategy aside.

At the end of his life, in 1863, he returned to this dilemma and tried a new solution. He now proposed that his partisans withdraw from the established social order and found new embryonic anarchist institutions. 'Since the old world rejects us', there is nothing to do but 'separate ourselves from it radically'.[38] United in their own organizations, the anarchists would demonstrate the merits of their theory and gradually win the vast majority to their cause.

Just why Proudhon thought withdrawal an appropriate strategy we will never know, because he died without working out its details. Certainly, it is morally legitimate, but that it is effective is less clear. Even if a majority were moved by a tactic of withdrawal to become anarchists, the problem would remain of dealing with the unconvinced minority. Proudhon suggests two methods. Occasionally he reverts to the bankrupt reliance on reasoned argument.[39] More often he urges the use of force. First anarchists must 'instill their ideas in the majority; having done this, they must capture political power by demanding control of its sovereign authority'.[40]

Proudhon's tactic of withdrawal may well come closer than any other he recommended to solving the anarchists' strategic dilemma, since it probably can go furthest toward reaching anarchy without coercion or fraud. But it is incapable, by itself, of achieving anarchy, as Proudhon, by recognizing that it could not sway everyone, admits. Hence an anarchist strategy both pure and effective had still not been discovered, even after Proudhon's extensive search.

BAKUNIN: THE PERILS OF FORCE AND FRAUD

Though Bakunin and Proudhon agree so much in their concepts of communal individuality that their visions of anarchy have here been considered to be essentially the same, on matters of strategy they are far apart. Bakunin, in fact, is more like Kropotkin than like Proudhon in his strategy, and Proudhon is more like Godwin than like Bakunin. For whereas Proudhon started out trusting to reason and only during temporary lapses or with agonized reluctance backed force or deception, Bakunin never relied exclusively on reason and in his strategy gave force and deception a substantial, permanent place.[41]

The paradoxical differences between the strategies of Bakunin and Proudhon can be partially explained as a response to disillusion and despair. As inventive and determined attempts to progress towards anarchy met repeated failure, even in revolutionary situations when prospects were best, anarchists became doubtful of ever achieving success. It is thus hardly surprising that Bakunin, who did not begin writing on anarchism until 1864, should have been less repelled than his more innocent predecessors by moral compromise. But there is a deeper reason, in his strategic premises, for Bakunin's greater reliance on coercion and deceit. Godwin and Proudhon had supposed that for the most part coercion and deceit were illegitimate *and* ineffective. Anarchists, they thought, must eschew these practices not only because they were impermissible, but also because they could not reach the end being sought. Bakunin's strategy is based on a contrary supposition. He believes that force and fraud, though illegitimate when viewed apart from their results, are still required in the many cases where they are needed to win victory. Bakunin's strategic thinking is largely an attempt to show how and when intrinsically immoral tactics are the ones anarchists must choose.

Most of the impure tactics Bakunin recommended were for revolutionary action, but one, the abolition of the right to inherit income-producing property, could be enacted by the state. There is, of course, no conflict between anarchist morality and the abolition of inheritance, provided the abolition is voluntary. But since Bakunin envisaged it as compelled by legal government, it is a tactic that anarchist ideals forbid.

What Bakunin recommended was that the state gradually limit and eventually repeal laws protecting inheritance, transfer the property accumulated by deceased owners to anarchist productive enterprises, and take the financial responsibility which had rested on parents for the education and upbringing of children. Contrary to the conventional wisdom, the right to inherit property was not needed as an incentive to work. Aversion to work arose from its being 'excessive, brutalizing and compulsory'; in an anarchist society it would be a basic need. Besides being a safe strategy, the legal abolition of inheritance was sure. Inherited wealth 'perpetuated inequality, the privileges of the few and the slavery of the many'. It therefore 'sufficed to abolish the right of inheritance in order to abolish the juridical family and the state'.[42]

This project for leading the state to suicide through its own legal enactments has a certain dramatic appeal, but its success is not to be expected. Marx put his finger on its foolishness. 'The whole thing rests on a superannuated idealism, which considers the actual jurisprudence as the basis of our economical state, instead of seeing that our economical state is the basis and source of our jurisprudence!'[43] Fortunately, though Bakunin never stopped riding his jurisprudential hobby horse, he worked out more serious strategies for revolutionary action. Following Godwin and Proudhon, he deemed most people irrational and ignorant. He followed them further in finding the source of this ignorance and irrationality in the inequality, legality and coercion of the established regime. And he also agreed that anarchy must be founded on nothing less than the majority's enlightened choice.[44] Yet though he agreed with his predecessors on all these points, he went much further than Proudhon toward recommending force and deceit as methods for enlightening the masses.

The premise on which his support for force and deceit rests is a belief in enlightenment through action. Proudhon, and especially Godwin, had sought enlightenment mainly through reasoned argument. For Bakunin, who believed that 'doctrine kills life', enlightenment could be found only through practical experience.[45] A majority would never be convinced by reasons to become anarchists, but their allegiance could be won by immersing them in a concerted, and perhaps violent, struggle against the state. Bakunin's schemes for this immersion were tied closely to the fluctuating political situation; they included the incitement by convinced anarchists of industrial strikes, peasant jacqueries and even full scale civil wars. But underlying his varied projects was the same strategic claim. Struggle against the state 'is always favorable to the awakening of the people's initiative and to their mental, moral and even their material development. The reason is simple: It shakes their sheepish disposition, so valuable to governments. . .It disrupts the brutalizing monotony of their daily life. . .and, by forcing them to consider the various pretensions of the princes or parties which compete for the right to oppress and exploit them, leads them to awareness, if not reflective, at least instinctive, of this profound truth: the rights of any government are as void as those of all the others, and their intentions are equally bad.'[46]

It is obvious that the strategy Bakunin here espouses often involves what is for anarchists the illegitimate use of force. Not all of the anarchists' struggles would require physical coercion, and Bakunin was anxious to limit its scope. He flatly rejected systematic terror and, perhaps wistfully, promised that 'there will be no need to destroy men'.[47] But his avowal of the need 'to be ruthless with positions and things' and the unavoidable coercion of his called-for civil war leave no doubt that anarchists, in their Bakuninist struggles, would sometimes combat opponents with physical force.[48]

Whether Bakunin's strategy also involves fraud is a more vexed question, whose answer depends on what he envisages as happening when anarchists immerse the masses in struggle. If the anarchists disclosed the full aim of this immersion, they could not be at all guilty of fraud. If they lied to the masses about the aim they were seeking, they would be blatant practitioners of deceit. But Bakunin avoids both of these clear alternatives by recommending a veiled, limited disclosure. The anarchists, though united in an active organization, are to conceal their membership from those they are trying to immerse. While explaining the short-range purpose of their effort, which is to satisfy particular, immediate grievances, their long-range purpose, to change society radically, is not to be revealed.[49] Since the masses, though not entirely fooled about the intended purpose of their struggle, would be deliberately misled about its chief aim, one must conclude that despite Bakunin's attempts at honesty he is still an espouser of fraud.

Though Bakunin's strategy is quite markedly imperfect, it

might still more adequately solve the anarchists' dilemma than the purer strategies of his predecessors. A sacrifice of perfection is not the same as a betrayal of anarchist ideals. If imperfect means could beget anarchy without causing too much suffering or loss of life, they would be a more faithful expression of its principles than pure but ineffective measures. The central issue in evaluating Bakunin's strategy is thus whether, by giving up perfection, his strategy gains enough effectiveness to justify its impurity.

In making this evaluation it is important to recognize that Bakunin gives up moral purity with caution. He is especially careful to protect relations within anarchist organizations from corruption. These organizations, being the nuclei for the good society, must be free of existing society's coercion, deceit and associated depravities. 'Otherwise, one would wind up with a political dictatorship, that is to say, with a reconstituted state, together with its privileges, its inequalities and all of its oppressions.'[50] To escape this fate, Bakunin insists on organizing an open anarchist movement, in small, autonomous units, without central leadership. He thus incorporates in his theory what is perhaps Godwin's crucial strategic insight: the members of an anarchy must grow apt for their new life, not after it is instituted, but while they build it.

It is in defining the relations between anarchists and the un-swayed masses that Bakunin's resistance to moral compromise deserts him, as we have seen, and it is the value of the limited though significant impurities he admits to these relations that now must be assessed. If Godwin was right that force and fraud in-variably 'confound the process of reason',[51] Bakunin's reliance on them could be dismissed summarily. But Godwin goes too far in his objection to force and fraud by claiming that they *always* damage reason. Occasionally they support it, as when used by careful educators to stimulate the minds of the unthinking. If force or deception has a modest scope, aims at the immediate growth of rationality, and has secured it in the past, it may be an appropriate strategy for anarchists. But Bakunin's coercive, deceptively incited struggle lacks all of these attributes. Its scope is a whole society; it aims to increase rationality indirectly, through a precarious chain of causes; it is untested by experience. There is thus no reason to expect that it would lead to anarchy. Since the success of the struggle Bakunin envisaged is not to be expected, he sacrificed perfection to no avail.

With the lessons of decades of failure to instruct him, and a synthetic ideal of communal individuality for guidance, Kropotkin is better situated to solve the dilemma of anarchist strategy than his predecessors. He does indeed avoid several of their most damaging pitfalls and bring a fresh perspective to his search. He even comes closer than the other anarchists to finding tactics both legitimate and sure. His failure to find them calls less for explanation than for answering the question to which the analysis in this chapter points of why a solution to the anarchists' dilemma is so difficult.

Kropotkin's strategy, like Bakunin's, calls for enlightenment through action, but owing mainly to a different supposition about the extent of rationality, it is less morally impure. He is at one with Bakunin in rejecting anarchism's early confidence in the *potential* capacity of the masses to reason. It is naive, he agrees, to expect the enormous growth of mental powers that Godwin, especially, had foreseen. But he differs from Bakunin on a point crucial for strategy by his greater confidence in popular reason's *actuality*. Progress in science has not, as Godwin thought, depended solely on the glorious discoveries of a few geniuses like Newton. It rests as well on the modest innovations of numerous obscure workers. History thus shows that ordinary people, far from being ignorant, are as great a source of progress as the intellectual elite.[52]

Believing in the present capacity of most people for clear thinking, Kropotkin proposes to treat them more forthrightly than had Bakunin. 'It offends the human spirit to immerse it in a destructive struggle unless it has a conception – if only rudimentary – of what will replace the world it is trying to destroy.'

Hence, instead of hiding the purpose of their effort, the anarchists must 'immediately lay out and discuss all aspects of [their] goal'. To do less would be to manipulate, and history shows that 'manipulators invariably betray the people'.[53] Unity of action comes not through guile, 'but through the unity of aims and the mutual confidence which never fail to develop when a great number of persons have consciously embraced a common ideal'.[54]

Kropotkin is also more wary than Bakunin of force. No anarchist, not even Godwin, entirely rejected physical coercion, and in his early years Kropotkin sometimes even advanced a limited defense of terror.[55] But his mature strategy has no place for the Bakuninist hope of achieving anarchy through coercion applied by persons blind to its point. Once again confidence in the present existence of rationality leads Kropotkin to strategic circumspection. Since most people are already tolerably apt thinkers, disclosing the real reasons why they should use force only makes its exercise more effective. Violent struggle is acceptable, but the strugglers must never be 'cast into the unknown without the support of a definite, clearly formulated idea to serve them as a springboard'.[56]

Kropotkin agrees with his predecessors in considering the historical development of government and inequality as a necessary preparation for achieving anarchy. Representative government, for example, 'has rendered service in the struggle against autocracy'. 'By its debates it has awakened public interest in public questions.' But now it is at best 'an anachronism, a nuisance'.[57] Since government and inequality have now completed their preparative service, the time has come for anarchists to replace them.

Since Kropotkin sees enlightenment as arising from both practice and theory, he proposes to reach anarchy through both action and thought. Following the early anarchists, he opts for reasoned argument, but he also takes from the later anarchists a preference for active struggle. Once the requisite historical conditions have been reached, there must be 'implacable criticism' of 'the accepted ideas of the constitution of the state'. This criticism must go on everywhere – not just among the learned – 'in drawing room as in cabaret, in the writing of philosophers as in daily conversation'.[58] But discussion among intimates, which for Godwin was a sufficient tactic, Kropotkin finds inadequate. And he adds significantly to anarchist strategy by showing a new way to stimulate subversive acts.

'Courage, devotion, the spirit of sacrifice, are as contagious as cowardice, submission and panic.' Armed with this conviction, which the emphasis on emotion in his ideal of communal individuality suggests, Kropotkin urges anarchists on to acts 'of illegal protest, of revolt, of vengeance'. What matter that these heroic deeds will not succeed at once. The anarchists are 'lonely sentinels, who enter the battle long before the masses are sufficiently roused'. 'The people secretly applaud their courage'; 'the revolutionary whirlwind...revives sluggish hearts'. Emotional contagion, though it passes through periods of incubation, is unstoppable; soon many will be seized by 'the spirit of revolt'.[59]

Will they form a majority? Kropotkin thought so at first. Later, he thought they would be 'a respectably numerous minority of cities and villages scattered over the country'.[60] But neither the morality nor the effectiveness of his strategy is much affected by whether, as a proportion of the population, the anarchists number fifty-one percent. When they predominate significantly, Kropotkin would have them carry out a thorough expropriation. By describing it in detail, he works out an aspect of anarchist strategy previously neglected: the steps to take *after* struggles have begun.

Kropotkin is not precise about how far anarchists should go toward abolishing legal government during the period of preliminary expropriation. Collective rule-making, perhaps resting on the preferences of majorities, would apparently be allowed, provided it was carried out in local workplaces and districts. But any rules enacted by these agencies, rather than being enforced physically, would from the start be enforced by means of censure. Kropotkin thus carries forward a theme introduced into the anarchist tradition by Godwin: though in a mature anarchy legal government must be totally abolished, it may continue to exist, in an attenuated form, during anarchy's preparatory phases.

Though Kropotkin is somewhat vague about the process for carrying out anarchist expropriation, he is specific about the changes it involves. He warns against confusing expropriation with confiscation, with impoverishing the rich by dividing up their wealth. No one would be deprived of articles of personal consumption, nor would capital be affected – except so far as it enabled 'any man...to appropriate the product of another's toil'.[61] The seizure of property would nevertheless be extensive. The insurgent anarchists must, through a rapid and complete takeover making no use of the nation state, assure everyone a reliable supply of life's necessities. Warehouses, factories, dwellings and farms all must be seized, inventoried and redistributed so as to satisfy needs and eliminate exploiters.[62] Expropriation would thus be eminently constructive. In seizing property the anarchists would at the same time reorganize the social infrastructure. Here the abstract call of Proudhon and Bakunin to build the new society by demolishing the state receives a plausible, concrete meaning.[63] In Kropotkin's expropriation destruction and creation appear reconciled.

Yet the possibility of conflict remains. How can one be sure that even Kropotkin's anarchists, though hard to tempt, would have the discipline, while expropriating, to resist taking personal possession of their seized wealth? Or, even if they resisted greed, would they be wise enough immediately to create a working anarchy? These are among the more embarrassing of the evaluative questions Kropotkin's strategy must face.

The truth is that despite his intrepid efforts to avoid both unnecessarily immoral tactics of Bakunin's sort and insufficiently vigorous tactics such as Godwin's, Kropotkin still fails to find a strategy both sure and legitimate. His strategy, stripped to essentials, rejects deception altogether and accepts coercion for just two purposes: to inspire the contagion of insurrectionary feeling and to carry out the seizure of accumulated productive wealth. The defects in this strategy are by now almost too familiar. Its avoidance of deception makes it ineffective; its acceptance of coercion makes it illegitimate, without giving it the means of success.

The spectacle of Godwin stumbling on the path to anarchy through reason is sufficient to discredit Kropotkin's utter rejection of fraud. Surely anarchists, to be successful, must follow Bakunin part way in sometimes, like ordinary politicians, being less than fully candid. By utterly rejecting deceptive tactics, Kropotkin greatly burdens his coercive ones. Feelings of daring would have to be farfetchedly contagious to spread as much in response to displays of force as Kropotkin needs them to. (And what of the destructive feelings that displays of force might spread?) The mass of expropriators would have to be improbably skilled and selfless to reorder society without leaders, without a unitary legal system and with no preconceived plan. Kropotkin, to be sure, tries to answer these objections, and not always by invoking popular rationality and good sense. Sometimes he uses an argument borrowed from radical democrats about the educative effects of direct local participation.[64] Sometimes he defends the 'discomfort and confusion' that would follow expropriation as being, 'for the mass of the people', still 'an improvement on their former condition. Besides, in times of Revolution one can dine contentedly enough on a bit of bread and cheese while eagerly discussing events.'[65] Is it unfair to see in this recourse to asceticism an admission by Kropotkin of strategic failure? Appearing as it does in the most confident of his mature works, it surely betrays uncertainty about the chance of his strategy's success. Kropotkin did come closer than any of his predecessors to finding an effective, legitimate strategy. But the soundness of the doubts he harbored about whether he had found one would be foolish to contest.

THE FUTILITY OF ANARCHIST STRATEGY

Daniel Guerin ends his sympathetic account of the anarchists' 'main constructive themes' with a confession. 'Relations between the masses and the conscious minority constitute a problem to which no full solution has been found by the Marxists or even by the anarchists, and one on which it seems that the last word has not yet been said.'[66] Guerin's partial acknowledgment of the anarchists' strategic failure is well supported by the evidence presented in this chapter. But this evidence indicates the need for a considerably more drastic portrayal of the anarchists' strategic plight. It is not only the problem of their relations to unconvinced outsiders that they fail to solve: the problems of how to organize internally and how, united with the masses, to proceed from old to new also baffle them. Nor are these problems whose solutions will, as Guerin implies, be found in the future. If the last word about them has not been said yet, this must be because there is none.

Part of the reason why anarchist strategy fails lies in the radicalism of its objective. Any theorist whose objective is as sweeping, abstractly defined and strongly opposed as the anarchists' will find his choice of means treacherous and unreliable. To reach a vast, vague end in the teeth of opposition calls for energetic, wide-ranging measures. Such measures are sure to have numerous unexpected consequences and may have none of the intended ones. Hence the goal sought will not be reached, or, if it is, it will be undermined by destructive side effects.[67] Rapid, wholesale change can certainly be warranted in situations where it is the alternative to great misery. But as a means of achieving radical aspirations it is very nearly doomed to fail.

If the vastness of the change needed to reach anarchy makes its achievement difficult, the special character of the needed change makes achieving it virtually impossible. The communal individuality that must flourish under anarchy involves personal traits, such as honesty and sympathy, and social traits, such as trust and cooperation, which, needing a stable peaceful climate, are put in special jeopardy by energetic measures. Yet anarchists must use such measures, unless they are willing to abandon hope. The genial humaneness of their aspirations thus burdens anarchists with an especially intractable version of the dilemma in which all radicals are caught.

That anarchist strategy is a failure cannot be proved beyond all doubt. Though no anarchist has yet found an auspicious strategy, and though the obstacles to finding one are immense, the bare possibility of success – for even the least promising – still must be acknowledged to exist. But judgments about the success of tactics, being dependent on contingencies, can never be fully certain. Anarchist strategy must be judged a failure, according to the appropriate measure of its probable success.

6

THE PLACE OF ANARCHISM IN THE SPECTRUM OF POLITICAL IDEAS

The ideas of anarchists, when compared with those of socialists or liberals, are often found to be essentially the same. Oscar Jaszi, for instance, sees 'the fundamental element of anarchism' as 'the extension of classical liberalism from the economic to all other fields', while Daniel Guerin, followed by Noam Chomsky, finds that 'the anarchist is primarily a socialist'.[1] This chapter shows, by subjecting these claims about the ideological place of anarchism to scrutiny, that neither can be effectively sustained. Anarchism is revealed as occupying its own distinct position in the spectrum of political ideas.

The elements of anarchist theory which will be found to set it apart from its close neighbors are its fundamental value and its view of the workings of the state. What separates anarchism from liberalism is its commitment to the value of community. What separates it from socialism is its ascription to the state's inherent attributes, such as its impersonality, of the most significant effects. Now socialists share the anarchists' commitment to community, while liberals share their ascription of the state's effects to its inherent attributes. Hence it is these two elements of anarchism in combination that mark it as unique. Were it not for the anarchists' commitment to community, they would have to be placed in the liberal camp. Were it not for their belief in the causal efficacy of the state's inherent attributes, they would have to be accounted socialists. But since anarchists are both communitarian in values and emphasizers of what is inherent in the workings of the state, their theory differs fundamentally from both of those with which it is most frequently confused.

The main purpose in comparing anarchism to socialism and liberalism is to clarify its structure as systematic thought. Its arguments stand out more boldly, when distinguished from those of kindred theories. But there is also a practical value to this comparison. So long as anarchism is thought equivalent at root to socialism or liberalism, different at most in being purer, what is at stake in choosing to be an anarchist is misperceived. Since a variant of familiar socialist or liberal beliefs seems all one must accept, the choice of anarchism appears quite trivial. But when anarchism is recognized as a separate theory, making bold, distinctive claims, the decision to be an anarchist stands revealed as daring.

ANARCHISM, LIBERALISM AND COMMUNITY

Of writers who think anarchists should be viewed as liberals, William E. Hocking is more elaborate than most in backing his claims with reasons. The main point of agreement between anarchists and liberals for Hocking is on the overriding value of freedom understood as the absence of coercion by the state. For anarchists as for liberals 'liberty. . .is the chief of all political goods'. As for their dispute about whether the state should be abolished, Hocking sees it as stemming from differences in psychology and thus of minor importance when compared to their agreement on first values. Liberals 'think that the self-seeking and deceitful elements in human nature will remain statistically about as they are', while anarchists 'believe in a moral progress such that the social casing of coercion may eventually be discarded'.[2] Both take the same position on the most basic issue in political theory – the nature of intrinsic value – and it is only differences on secondary, psychological matters that lead to their dramatic, yet superficial disagreement on the wisdom of abolishing the state.

The main trouble with this argument for seeing anarchists as liberals is that it misconstrues the position of both groups on which values are ultimate. Hocking shares the misconception of anarchists as committed above all to freedom from the state, which was dispelled in Chapter 3 and replaced by the view that their chief goal is communal individuality. What must be added here is that freedom is not even the chief goal for all liberals.

Many liberals do, of course, embrace it. Kant, for instance, called freedom 'the one sole and original right that belongs to every human being by virtue of his humanity'. And he means nothing complicated or paradoxical by freedom, in this context, at any rate: it is 'independence from the constraint of another's will'.[3] Equally frank expressions of commitment to freedom thus defined can be found in the writings of other leading liberals, such as Benjamin Constant.[4]

But these statements do not prove that for all liberals such freedom has supreme intrinsic worth. For utilitarian liberals, including Bentham, and perhaps Mill, its value is instrumental.[5] These theorists set value on freedom only as a means to happiness and not as an end in itself. Should freedom conflict with happiness, utilitarian liberals are bound logically to oppose it, and if happiness is increased by state coercion they must give such coercion their support.

The claim that anarchists are liberals is thus easily refuted, so far as it presumes that freedom from state coercion is the chief good for both groups. But this refutation is not invincible. Liberals and anarchists do agree in opposing coercive government. Though the normative basis for this agreement is not the shared commitment to freedom alleged by writers such as Hocking, this does not mean that liberals and anarchists base their opposition on different norms. While not sharing the supreme value usually ascribed to them, they still might share one, which serves for both as the basis for their opposition to the state.

One value used by liberals as a basis for objecting to state coercion is autonomy, understood as acting from no empirical motive, but for the sake of duty. Kant objected to state coercion on this ground when he noted that the incentive to comply with 'juridical legislation, . . .being different from the idea of duty itself, must derive from pathological grounds determining the will, that is, from inclinations'.[6] Since an action, to be autonomous in the Kantian sense, must be done for duty's sake, and since fear is the motive for acceding to state coercion, such coercion is reprehensible.

It is easy to show that none of the anarchists we are considering use Kantian autonomy as the normative basis for their opposition to state coercion. Godwin, Bakunin and Kropotkin do not, because they are determinists who deny the possibility of choice uncaused by inclinations.[7] Though Proudhon seems to admit this possibility, he does not elevate it to the status of supreme good. It need not have even instrumental worth, since he prizes right but empirically determined choices more highly than choices that are wrong but empirically undetermined.

Another value to which liberals appeal in their objections to state coercion is utility. It is on this basis that Bentham writes: 'All punishment is itself an evil', because 'it tends to subtract from. . .happiness'.[8] Punishment, the most typical form of state coercion, definitionally causes its victims to suffer pain. Utility mandates the maximization of satisfaction. Hence, if utility is the supreme value, then punishment, and the state that inflicts it, stand at least presumptively condemned.

There is enough ambiguity in the attitude of some anarchists toward the principle of utility to make calling them utilitarians seem plausible. Godwin is especially easy to treat in this way, since he repeatedly praises satisfaction as the supreme good. As for his seemingly contrary words of praise for other goods, particularly community and individuality, these need not be read as ascriptions of supreme value, but may be construed as empirical statements about how the most satisfaction can be achieved. Godwin can then be said to approve of these other goods as means to utility rather than as equal to it in worth.[9]

It is possible to give a similar interpretation of Kropotkin, whose agreement with the utilitarians is shown clearly by his way of framing the question to be solved by anarchism: 'What forms of social life assure to a given society, and then to mankind generally, the greatest amount of happiness?'[10] No doubt, he, like Godwin, approves of goods other than satisfaction. But his approval for these goods may be seen as instrumental, arising from their richness as utility's source.

Calling Kropotkin a subscriber to utilitarianism is indefensible because he goes out of his way to condemn that doctrine as framed by its founders. He faults Bentham for 'the incompleteness of his ethics' and Mill for the absence from his theory of 'the principle of justice'.[11] What Kropotkin is here alluding to is the commonplace among critics of utilitarianism that an action which maximizes satisfaction may still be wrong. Since we condemn actions which utility tells us to approve, utility cannot always be of overriding worth.

It is harder to show the error in calling Godwin a utilitarian. His praise for the principle of utility is nowhere counterweighed by criticism, and he takes pains to reconcile this praise empirically with his avowals of support for rival goods. Yet one cannot avoid suspecting that his attempt at reconciliation fails. His claims about the effectiveness of community and individuality as a means to happiness are much exaggerated. Would he ever stop approving them in cases where it seemed likely that their opposites, such as deceit or servile deference, would advance utility more? Though Godwin's utilitarianism is formally consistent, its empirical contestability casts its plausibility into doubt.

But Godwin's utilitarianism, even if authentic, is insufficient evidence that anarchists agree with liberals in using the greatest happiness principle to criticize the state. Though Bakunin is silent on the merit of utilitarianism, Proudhon denounces it even more emphatically than Kropotkin does. 'It cannot be said that everything...useful...is just; in case of conflict the choice is indisputable, justice is entitled to command.'[12] Proudhon is here making Kropotkin's familiar point: utility may sanction wrongful acts. But he goes beyond this commonplace, with his characteristic rigor, when he proclaims: 'Right and interest are two things as radically distinct as debauchery and marriage.'[13] A more thoroughgoing renunciation of utilitarian morality is difficult to conceive.

There is one other value to which liberals appeal in their objections to state coercion which seems more promising than autonomy or utility as a mark of normative agreement with anarchism. This value is individuality of the kind prized by

J. S. Mill. It is a main part of Mill's case against coercive government that it debilitates the character of rulers and ruled alike, when it silences opinion, prevents self-regarding action, or benevolently interferes by giving too much help. State coercion is for Mill a menace to the individuality, understood as energetic personality, that he prizes as the supreme element in human worth.

Individuality, of course, as we have seen in Chapter 3, also has intrinsic value for the anarchists. When Godwin calls it 'the very essence of human excellence', he sounds like Mill's anticipator.[14] When Kropotkin demands its 'most complete development' he sounds like Mill's disciple.[15] Texts of Proudhon and Bakunin also could be cited to show that in setting inherent value on individuality and in appealing to it in their arguments against the state, all four anarchists agree with Mill – the quintessential liberal. This agreement would seem to give the basis, which Hocking failed to find, for claiming anarchists as liberals. Though freedom cannot be cited as the value used by both groups to condemn coercive government, individuality can be. And since anarchists and liberals share this basic value, their theories, one might argue, must be regarded as at root the same.

The main trouble with this attempt to save Hocking's thesis is that it overlooks the difference in normative status assigned by the two groups to community. Anarchists do not prize individuality *simpliciter*: communal individuality is their goal. Their project, we have learned, is to organize society so as to maximize individuality *and* community seen as equal, interdependent values. Liberals give community a lower status. For some it is an interference with the satisfaction, freedom or individuality they most prize. For others it is normatively irrelevant. Thinking of society as a device to protect intrinsic values, they regard it as an instrument and are indifferent to the reciprocity of awareness among its members called community.[16] The value of community, which for anarchists is inherent, is thus for liberals instrumental at most. This disagreement between the two groups in normative starting point is decisive evidence for the conclusion defended here. Anarchists, far from being an especially hardy breed of liberals, are an entirely different race.

The commitment of anarchists to community is significant as more than a mark setting them apart from liberals. It also provides an explanation, more convincing than is usual, for their disagreement with liberals on the wisdom of abolishing the state. The standard explanation for this disagreement, mentioned above, relies on alleged differences between the two groups on the possibilities of human nature. The weakness of this explanation is that they actually agree closely on these possibilities. Thus, their difference in first values is extremely fortunate for explaining why they disagree about whether the state should be abolished. If both groups proceeded from the same first values, their disagreement on this issue would be much harder to explain.

Liberal psychologies all lack two antithetical assumptions about human nature that are often found in political theory. On the one hand, they do not consider any vicious motive such as the desire to oppress or cause suffering to be irremediably and universally dominant. Nor do they concede the possibility that a benevolent motive might achieve this status. Within the limits set by these omissions, liberals adopt a variety of psychologies ranging from Locke's relatively benign one to Bentham's hedonism, and including intermediate positions such as Kant's 'asocial sociability'.[17] But here the subject is not differences among liberal psychologies, but similarities. Anarchists agree with liberals in upholding what is common to the liberal outlook, since they too deny both that malevolence is always dominant everywhere and that the universally dominant motive can be benevolence.

Human nature as described by Proudhon lies clearly within the boundaries of liberal psychology. He explicitly rejects the same two hypotheses about motivation as the liberals, while in his own psychology, man, suspended between these extremes, 'may be defined with equal justice as either a pugnacious animal or a sociable one'.[18] Bakunin holds a similarly liberal view concerning the motivational weight of kindness as compared with malice. Man, for Bakunin, has 'two opposed instincts, egoism and sociability', neither of which predominates, for 'he is both more ferocious in his egoism than the most ferocious beasts and more sociable than bees and ants'.[19]

Godwin and Kropotkin are less easily characterized in their psychologies as liberal. The problem, of course, lies not in the pessimism of these theorists about the future of malevolence, but in their optimism about the possibilities of human kindness. It is not hard to show, however, that the reputations of Godwin and Kropotkin as naive believers in benevolence are caricatures.[20]

As part of his campaign against psychological egoism Godwin does insist on the force of kindly motives. Nor can it be denied that he expects them to become stronger, more impartial and more widespread in the future, as social conditions are improved. But these claims do not amount to the thesis, frequently ascribed to him, that benevolence can become universally predominant. Often, he says the opposite. A late work, *Thoughts on Man*, calls 'the love of power' a motive which 'never entirely quits us'. It portrays man as 'a creature of mingled substance'. And it warns solemnly against the 'few men in every community that are sons of riot and plunder'.[21] Lest these professions of doubt on the prospects of benevolence be thought symptoms of Godwin's old age, it should be noted that they also appear in the earlier and more optimistic *Political Justice*. Godwin there advances the doctrine of perfectibility, which for him includes progress in benevolence. But he is careful to delineate the limits to perfectibility, of which the most important is intractable human nature. So 'shut in on all sides' is man by the 'limited nature of the human faculties' that it would be pretence for him to 'lay claim to absolute perfection'.[22] Since we will never be perfect, benevolence will not always be our strongest motive. Thus, not even in his most optimistic work did Godwin's faith in human kindness surpass the liberals'.

Kropotkin's position on the future of benevolence is much the same. He too stresses the actual force of motives such as love and devotion. He too claims that under anarchy these motives will be stronger and more widespread. But no more than Godwin does he regard them as potentially predominant. In his description of anarchy not everyone is kindly. 'Certain among us' will still be governed by 'anti-social instincts'.[23] Kropotkin, like Godwin, sees more potentialities for benevolence than Proudhon or

Bakunin. But his confidence in it is slight enough to serve along with Godwin's as conclusive evidence that in their estimates of human nature anarchists and liberals agree.

The agreement between anarchists and liberals in psychology makes the main problem of their politics the same. By denying that malevolence is ineradicable, both rule out autocracy as a mode of organization. For only if viciousness must be widespread and rampant is autocracy needed to safeguard peace. By denying the possibility of universal benevolence, they also rule out as unworkable modes of organization which exert no cohesive force. For only if kindliness is the overriding motive, can an utterly spontaneous society exist. Thus the problem of politics for anarchists and liberals alike is to describe a pattern of social relations that, without being autocratic, provides the required cohesive force.

There are two ways to solve this problem.[24] The first, the choice of liberals, is to accept, and limit, the coercive state. Anarchists choose the second solution, familiar from earlier chapters of this book: they reject the state entirely and rely instead on public censure. It is the disagreement between the two groups in normative starting point that explains the difference in how they solve their common problem. Both groups regard the legal form and coercive sanctions, which are inherent in the state, as causing its most important effects. But whereas the anarchists' commitment to community leads them to evaluate these effects so negatively that they reject all states, even the most limited, and turn instead to public censure, liberals are led by their indifference to community to a more positive evaluation, which encourages them to reject censure and to admit the need for a limited state.

Liberals, in their denunciation of the state, often seem as adamant as anarchists. But some of their more vivid criticism is deceptive bluster. Paine, for instance, sounds anarchistically outraged as he berates 'the greedy hand of government, thrusting itself into every corner and crevice of industry, and grasping the spoil of the multitude'.[25] But his objection here, like many raised by liberals, is to a remediable excess, and thus no sign of categorical hostility. Being directed at avoidable shortcomings, rather than inherent defects, such objections serve not to destroy but to improve the state, by showing how to limit it so that it rules more gently. But besides their numerous contingent criticisms, liberals have at least two which, being aimed at the state's inherent attributes, are basic. The first of these criticisms is Bentham's, already mentioned, that punishment causes pain. This is an objection to an unavoidable defect inherent in all governments, since none can refrain from punishing altogether. The other liberal objection to an inherent attribute of the state is Kant's, also encountered before, that, owing to its unavoidable coercion, the incentive to obey a government may be fear of punishment. Since an autonomous action is done for the sake of duty, obedience to a government often lacks moral worth.

But though liberals object to some consequences of the state's coercion, they are prevented by their indifference to the value of community from assailing it with the anarchists' sort of all-out criticism. State coercion, for the anarchist, is more than painful, more than immoral. It is a poison which, by contaminating social relations with distrust, resentment and remote impersonality, causes community's dissolution. Here then is one way the difference between anarchists and liberals in fundamental values explains their disagreement about abolishing the state. The anarchists' commitment to the value of community gives them an emplacement, unavailable to liberals, from which to attack the effects of state coercion more forcefully.

It is not only because their criticism of state coercion is milder that liberals disagree with anarchists about its abolition. They also disagree because they outweigh their criticism with reverence for another of the state's inherent attributes, the rule of law. So prized by liberals are the consequences of law's familiar traits – its generality, stability and externality – that the bad effects of state coercion are overshadowed in their eyes, when it has these legal merits. The generality of law guards against practices liberals loathe, such as discrimination against eccentrics and exploitation by officials. Law's stability gives it a predictability esteemed by liberals as a source both of independence and satisfaction. And they prize law's externality for the protection it affords against governmental interference with private states of mind.

This outline of the liberal defense of law and thus the state, though sketchy, is sufficient for explaining why anarchists do not use it. For this purpose, the crucial point about this defense is its logical dependence on liberal values. It is the liberals' commitment to freedom, autonomy, individuality and utility that makes them find the effects of law desirable enough to outweigh the harm caused by state coercion. To anarchists, on the other hand, with their commitment to community, veneration of legality seems outrageous. As the comparison worked out early in this book between the anarchists' views of law and censure showed, from their communitarian perspective law, far from redeeming coercion, only makes it more repulsive. Being general, law ignores the individual diversities from which anarchist community draws its strength. Being permanent, it is too rigid as a regulator of communal ties. And being external, it is blind to community's very substance: the knowledge shared by all its members of the others' minds. Their commitment to community thus accounts for the anarchists' disagreement with liberals over the state's abolition by explaining not only why they attack the state more harshly, but also why they reject liberal arguments for state coercion redeemed by legal probity.

There is one other reason why liberals disagree with anarchists about abolishing the state: they oppose using public censure as the state's replacement. The degree to which the liberals oppose censure varies, depending on their attitude toward utilitarianism. Bentham, as a consistent utilitarian, finds no inherent fault in censure, but he finds no inherent merit in it either. Its value lies largely in its effectiveness as a behavioral control, concerning which he has grave doubts. That is why he includes it in his list of sanctions – calling it the moral or popular sanction – but relies on it very little in his proposals for reform.[26] Non-utilitarian liberals oppose censure forthrightly, as an unavoidable threat to their first values. Mill, interpreted as assigning individuality intrinsic worth, is the best known example of a liberal who rejects censure categorically. But Constant does so too, when he proclaims: 'we are modern men who want to develop our faculties as we please...and who have no use for authority except to obtain from it the general means of instruction it can provide'.[27] Since censure unavoidably obstructs self-development, it is as impermissible for Constant as for Mill.

Anarchists, of course, share the concern of liberals for the development of individuality. Yet they take issue with them by espousing censure, despite their recognition that for self-development it is a threat. Here too the explanation for the disagreement between the two groups is the difference in their fundamental values. Liberals reject censure, because the dearth of reciprocal awareness in the legal state means that admonishment by neighbors there can only cramp the self. But the bonds of community in the stateless environment of the anarchists make censure's effect on individuality more benign. Censure under anarchy is remarkable, we have learned, for the extent to which, owing largely to the communal context in which it operates, it nurtures human faculties by controlling behavior with reasons. It is because anarchists affirm the worth of communal understanding that they are able, unlike liberals, to give censure their support. For communal understanding provides them with a safeguard, unavailable to liberals, with which to check censure's destructive tendencies. Thus their difference in normative starting points is as sound as explanation for why anarchists disagree with liberals by praising public censure as for why they disagree with them by condemning coercion and law. The anarchists' communitarian commitment and its rejection by the liberals are the grounds to which all aspects of their disagreement about whether the state should be abolished must finally be traced.

The account advanced here of the deep difference between anarchism and liberalism clarifies what is at stake in choosing between them. It is not uncommon for liberals, who often see their relationship to anarchists in Hocking's terms, to claim an easy sympathy with anarchism as morally appealing but empirically unsound. The allegiance to liberal values they find in anarchism makes it seem congenial. But its unfortunate naivety concerning human nature marks it with an unacceptable extravagance. Thus liberals treat anarchism with both reverence and disdain, as a flawed but noble version of the truth.[28] There is a double mistake behind such treatment, we now can see, for the basic values of anarchism and liberalism differ, while their views of human nature are the same. Hence the choice between them turns not on disavowing an outlandish psychology, but on embracing a distinctive norm. This choice cannot be easy, since the norms of liberals and those of anarchists have a powerful but opposite appeal.

ANARCHISM, SOCIALISM AND THE STATE AS CAUSE

The boundary between anarchism and socialism cannot lie on the terrain of values, because communal individuality is the over-riding goal for both. Eccentric minor socialists such as Cabet can be cited, for whom community eclipses individuality as a source of worth, but an individualized community is the goal of the main socialist tradition, as exemplified by its profound, influential members, above all Marx.[29] Hence though an analysis of values has set anarchists apart from liberals, they must be marked off from socialists on some other ground. The point in their theories that sets anarchists and socialists apart most fundamentally is one on which anarchists and liberals agree: the importance as a source of consequences of the state's inherent attributes.

Having traced the anarchists' abhorrence of law and government to their distinctive normative commitment, we must be startled to find that socialists, though sharing this commitment, nevertheless endorse the state, not only as a means to build the good society, but as one of that society's integral parts. That socialists rely on the state tactically, whether by seizing it with force or claiming it with votes, is a longstanding commonplace.[30] That they also incorporate it into their good society is more contestable, especially in light of what Marx and Engels say about its ultimate disappearance. Yet it is easy to show that the Marxist good society, even at its highest stage, includes elements of legal government which are banned from a mature anarchy.

Marx and Engels, in their remarks about the state's future, do not say that it will disappear entirely; rather, they mention certain of its particular attributes, qualified as political, which alone are destined to die out.[31] Included among these are its use as a 'government of persons' and as an instrument of 'class rule', or 'special repressive force'.[32] What Marx and Engels mean to designate by the last two of these phrases is fairly clear: no force will be used by officials in the ultimate phase of socialism to weaken or eliminate opponents. For in the ultimate phase of socialism, since there will be no more classes, there will be no opponents for officials to repress. As for the disappearance of a 'government of persons', this must be seen in the light of its replacement, 'the administration of things'. Thus considered, it means an end to the legal regulation of behavior, except when needed to protect efficiency. The members of the classless society will be so cooperative that legal government will not have to prevent crime.

Besides enumerating the attributes of the state that will become outmoded, Marx and Engels also mention some that will remain. Elections, for example, though they will 'completely lose their political character', will still occur under socialism. And though the officials chosen at these elections will perform no 'governmental functions', 'general functions' such as supervising the economy will continue to be their task.[33] Thus Marx and Engels are at one with the mainstream of the socialist tradition in giving the state permanence. For the regulative institutions which they include in socialist society, despite the withering or transcendence they undergo, retain enough traces of legal authority to qualify as a state.[34]

The disagreement between anarchists and socialists concerning the abolition of the state is both a ground for suspecting that their theories differ and a source of puzzlement. Anarchists and socialists are both committed to communal individuality. Yet only anarchists use this shared commitment to justify the state's elimination. What is it about socialism that prevents its adherents from drawing out from the normative starting point they share with anarchists the anarchists' extreme anti-state conclusion? An answer to this question will clearly delineate the line that separates their theories.

There is no widespread reverence for legality among socialists which could serve, as it does for liberals, to explain their liking for the state. Some socialists, especially those with revisionist or Fabian sympathies, do show a liberal appreciation for the law's blessings. But neutrality or indifference toward the law as such is socialism's usual stance. For most socialists legal institutions draw their value not from their intrinsic character, but from the society that shapes them and from the interests that they serve. Nor can the liking of socialists for the state be explained by their view of human nature, since their pessimism about the future of benevolence is no greater than the anarchists'. Marx, of course, thought history was 'nothing but a continuous transformation of human nature'.[35] The place to look for an explanation of their differences concerning the abolition of the state is their analysis of its significance compared to the economy as a social cause.

All anarchists take note of a point much emphasized by socialists – how economic relations affect our lives for ill or good. Kropotkin, writing in a period that was obsessed by economics, goes further than his predecessors in tracing personal degradation and social mistrust to the baneful effects of a disordered economy, which he sees as causing damage not only directly, but also indirectly, through being a source of legal government. Kropotkin also works out more fully how the future economy will cause communal individuality to grow. But even Godwin's analysis of the economy's causal role includes the gist of Kropotkin's points. 'The spirit of oppression, the spirit of servility, and the spirit of fraud, these are the immediate growth of the established administration of property.' 'The unequal distribution of property' is also 'one of the original sources of government'. And an egalitarian economy would help to create a situation in which 'each man would be united to his neighbor, in love and mutual kindness. . .but each man would think and judge for himself'.[36] There is nothing in these affirmations with which a socialist need disagree.

Where anarchists and socialists part company is on the causal role of the state. Much of their disagreement on this subject is no more than a matter of degree or emphasis. Thus, while both groups recognize the effects of government on economic institutions, anarchists insist on them more.[37] And while both see that government, despite being affected by the economy, acts somewhat independently from it, anarchists insist more strongly on this independence.[38] But there is one question regarding the state as cause on which anarchists and socialists completely disagree: whether the state's inherent nature is a source of its effects. All of the state's effects are seen by socialists as arising from its particular, changeable attributes, mainly, in the Marxist case, its class character. Each government, for the Marxist, gets its most causally significant attributes from the relations of production which it reflects. Anarchists, on the other hand, while they certainly appreciate how the particular effects of each state are shaped by its changeable attributes, also emphasize, in contradistinction to the socialists, how its legality and coerciveness, which are inherent in its nature, constantly cause more serious effects. Thus Godwin implores us never to 'forget, that government is, abstractly taken, an evil, an usurpation upon the private judgment and individual conscience of mankind'. Bakunin maintains that 'despotism lies less in the *form* of the state or of power than in their very *principle*'. And Proudhon gives the anarchist analysis of the state as cause practical application in explaining his vote against one of France's most democratic constitutions: 'I voted against the Constitution, because it is a Constitution.'[39] For the anarchist, then, it makes no difference, so far as concerns its more important effects, who runs the state, how it is organized, or what it does. It debases and estranges its subjects regardless of these contingencies, just because it is a state.

With this understanding of the basic difference between anarchists and socialists to rely on, new meaning can be given to their well-known tactical disputes. The dramatic clashes between anarchists and socialists, which arose within the First International and have continued wherever anarchists have been politically significant, are conventionally seen as clashes over the bearing of circumstances on the effectiveness of the state as a means for reaching a mutually accepted goal. This interpretation is inadequate on at least two scores.

For one thing, its claim that the goal of anarchists and socialists is identical can only be accepted with stricter qualifications than are normally imposed. It is often said that the goal shared by socialists and anarchists is a self-regulating, classless society, bereft of government and law. Socialists, to be sure, see this goal as an ultimate end, while for anarchists it is an immediate objective, but its status as their shared goal can hardly be impugned by the fact that they plan to reach it on different schedules. This standard way of claiming that anarchists and socialists share goals fails because it ignores the disagreement between them just analyzed concerning the permanence of the state. Socialists and anarchists cannot possibly have the same goal, understood as a vision of the good society, because socialists give law and government a permanent place even in their good society's final stage. But though the claim that anarchists and socialists share goals is unacceptable in its standard version, properly qualified it holds up. Provided they are regarded not as a vision of a good society, but as values which a good society must express, the goals of anarchists and socialists are certainly identical, since communal individuality is the regulative value for both groups.

The other score on which the usual interpretation of the clash on tactics between anarchists and socialists must be questioned is its contention that the clash is over the issue of how the state's suitability as an instrument is affected by circumstances. When socialists rely on the state tactically, they do so, in this view, out of the belief that circumstances make it a helpful means for achieving victory. Anarchists arrive at their tactical opposition to the state by the same sort of reasoning. But their reading of the circumstances which socialists see as making the state a handy conveyance leads them to see it as a vehicle for reaching nothing but defeat. There is evidence in the writings of both groups to support this way of understanding their clash on tactics.

Socialists, with insignificant exceptions, agree that one way to win control of the state, in the right circumstances, is by taking title to it in an election. Marx, for instance, thinks that if there is universal suffrage, if capitalism is well-developed, if agriculture is industrialized, if there is no strong authoritarian tradition,

socialists should contest elections, because a majority of dedicated voters, who will support the desired social transformation,
can then be won.[40] Anarchists reject this strategy by denying that
the circumstances which socialists find auspicious give elections
even scanty promise. The mass of voters in present society are so
ignorant, so deferential, and so resigned that there is no hope of
attracting the support of a majority.[41]

The other way suggested by socialists for winning control of the
state is some sort of forceful seizure. Their projects for this seizure
(and hence their views about its needed circumstances) vary,
ranging from Blanqui's schemes for conspiracy by a small group
to Marx's hints at an open, broadly based insurrection. Circumstances which socialists see as affecting the success of a forceful
seizure pertain to such matters as the strength of the established
government, the disposition of the underlying population and the
capacities of the insurrectionary leadership. It is mainly concerning the last of these that anarchists and socialists part company.
Socialists believe that insurrectionary leaders, whether because of
their exemplary character, their dependence on their followers,
or their loyalty to their class, may have enough resolve selflessly
to build the good society once they have won power. Anarchists
deny this on the ground that the temptations of power are too
great. Not even the most dedicated revolutionary can be trusted
to build the good society, if he occupies a public office.[42]

It should be clear from this comparison that the usual account
of the clash between anarchists and socialists on tactics, which
traces it to their different assessments of attendant circumstances,
provides a workable explanation of their dispute. But this
explanation is superficial, because it makes no reference to the
deeper difference between them, brought out earlier in this
section, concerning the causal efficacy of the state's inherent
attributes. Even if they endorsed the socialists' favorable reading of circumstances, anarchists would not accept their tactical
reliance on the state, because, no matter how favorable the
circumstances in which it is used, the state for anarchists remain
a Moloch. It is only by recognizing the bearing on their familiar
tactical disputes of their disagreement concerning the state as

cause that the theoretical significance of these disputes can be appreciated. They are then revealed as more than wrangles over the empirical assessment of contingencies, for they are rooted in a difference antecedent to such wrangles about whether contingencies can ever be decisive, in judging the state's effects.

The error of those who claim that anarchists are socialists at heart stems from blindness toward their disagreement about the causal efficacy of the state *qua* state. A typical version of this claim is advanced by Noam Chomsky. Anarchism is not to be identified with socialism *simpliciter*, since many socialists rely on legal government. But there are also socialists (Chomsky cites Anton Pannekoek and William Paul) who are at one with anarchists in finding the state antipathetic. It is as part of this 'libertarian wing of socialism' that Chomsky thinks anarchism should be classed.[43]

If the antipathy to legal government of council communists, syndicalists and similar representatives of socialism's libertarian wing came from alarm about the effects of the state's inherent attributes, Chomsky's claim that anarchism is a type of socialism would be correct. But even the most libertarian of the socialists is alarmed mainly by effects of the state's changeable characteristics, such as its organization or policies. This difference in the causal perspective from which they view the state puts socialists, however libertarian, a great distance away from anarchists. What libertarian socialists find fault with in their criticism of the present state is not its impersonality or coercion, but its use by minorities to subjugate the many. What they fear in the state envisaged by a less libertarian socialism is not the perpetuation of an unredeemable institution, but its continued use as an oppressive instrument by a bureaucracy or a vanguard party. And what they project as a successor to the existing state is not a society freed of legal government, but a society organized, in Chomsky's words, 'on truly democratic lines, with democratic control in the workplace and in the community'.[44]

The same conclusion emerges from this comparison at every point. Libertarian socialists, mainly because of their oblivion to the state's permanent effects, are not anarchists, but democrats.

They want a system built on a pattern like that described by Paul, with industry 'democratically owned and controlled by the workers electing directly from their own ranks industrial administrative committees'.[45] Anarchists, to be sure, regard democracy as more progressive than other forms of government; some go so far as to give it a significant place in their strategy. But even a democracy purged of all bourgeois elements – impeccably participatory, thoroughly decentralized, genuinely industrial, proceeding entirely from the bottom up – produces the effects for which the anarchists condemn the state. Hence any theory such as libertarian socialism which, far from excluding democratic institutions from its vision of the good society, regards them as indispensable, cannot possibly be called anarchist.

We must thus conclude that even between anarchists and socialists whose affinities are closest, there is a clear dividing line. For the disagreement about the significance of the state as cause, which underlies their dispute about the future of democracy, overshadows the affinity arising from their shared antipathy to particular states. When libertarian socialists denounce the present state as a tool of capitalism, call for workers' councils, or attack elitism and bureaucracy, they may sound like anarchists, but in its relevant causal presuppositions the theory they depend on for reaching these conclusions is no form of anarchism at all.

If the usual view of the relationship between anarchism and socialism were acceptable, choosing between them would be a matter of empirical judgment. One need only decide which group, in assessing the state's effectiveness in varied circumstances, makes the more reliable predictions. Matters such as the anarchists' tendency to underestimate the educative effects of democracy and the socialists' tendency to underestimate the corrupting effects of power would have to be examined. When all the differences between the two groups which affect the reliability of their predictions had been weighed together, the balance on which the choice between them depended would be struck.

But the view presented here of where anarchism and socialism disagree shows that the choice between them rests on another

The place of anarchism

consideration. The world of politics has a different structure for the two groups, at least so far as it is composed of states. Socialists think that the state's significance as a source of political effects arises from its contingent attributes and from the causal nexus in which these attributes exist. For anarchists, the state's political significance lies elsewhere – in its independent, self-contained, unchangeable existence. Hence the choice between anarchism and socialism depends not on an empirical comparison, but on an ontological inquiry, not on the weighing of probabilities, at which socialists may be shrewder, but on the elucidation of conjectures, at which neither side is obviously better.

THE SINGULARITY OF ANARCHISM

The allegiance of the anarchists to both communal individuality and to viewing the state as an inherent cause not only makes their theory singular by distinguishing it from its close neighbors, but also accounts for its most noticeable peculiarities. In studying the anarchists we have continually found their commitment to communal individuality revealing. Their reliance on public censure, their search for mediation between individuals and groups, their radical social criticism and their fruitless quest for an effective strategy have all been illuminated when seen as shaped by the requirements of their guiding value. Yet since socialists as well as anarchists affirm this value, it cannot by itself account for what is distinctive about anarchism. Communal individuality as affected by anarchism's conception of the state as an inherent cause is what lies at the root of its peculiarities. Conceiving of the state as a malevolent god, drawing its power from its inner resources, anarchists, at all phases of their theorizing, must fight not only *for* their guiding value, but *against* their mortal enemy. It is because they strive for a communal individuality devoid of legal government that anarchists reach such peculiar conclusions about tactics and social structure. Less novel options are unavailable, being foreclosed by their conception of the causal efficacy of the state. Hence the singularity of anarchist theory lies not only in its defining attributes, but also in the contours

132

which these attributes shape. The characteristics of anarchism which set it apart from its close neighbors are also poles which inflect the course of its argument with attractive and repellent force. To redeem society on the strength of rational, spontaneous relations, while slaying the leviathan who offers minimal protection – this is the anarchist's daring choice.

7

EVALUATING ANARCHISM

Accurate understanding has been the main purpose of the previous chapters of this book, which have sought to elucidate the arguments of the anarchists faithfully and in detail. But accurate understanding is not this study's only purpose; another is evaluation. How consistent is the case for anarchism? What is its plausibility, if not its truth? And what is the moral value of its model of an ideal social order?

Fortunately, the foregoing analysis makes it unnecessary to answer these questions from scratch. For though this analysis has been expository, it has done more than describe. The process of establishing what anarchists are saying has included evaluation of their arguments with regard to both consistency and plausibility. We have found the anarchists to be unexpectedly consistent, with the sovereign value of communal individuality lending their arguments a marked unity. The plausibility of their arguments has also been substantiated. The anarchists, we have discovered, evince a certain realism about the obstacles posed by human nature, social conditions and the power of their adversaries to the success of their project. Since two of the evaluative questions which need to be addressed have already received direct attention, the assessment of the anarchists in this concluding chapter will be devoted mainly to the question, which so far has been slighted, of the value of their social model as a model of the best regime.

The gist of anarchy has been identified in this book as a society which, by virtue of its statelessness and its internal structure, provides utmost communal individuality and freedom. Anarchy may therefore be considered as a possible alternative to the

A complete achievement

models of a good society which more familiar political theories advance. The moral value of anarchy, viewed as a candidate for choice as the ideal social order, depends partly on its merit as a complete achievement, and partly on its merit as a critical standard and practical guide. It thus must be evaluated here from both of these perspectives.

ANARCHY AS A COMPLETE ACHIEVEMENT

No ideal society attains perfection, because the merits of each incur a moral price. Even the most attractive requires the sacrifice or abridgment of some values, because they are incompatible or uneasy with it. A society like Rousseau's, for example, which achieves equal political participation, can secure neither the material abundance of Marx's good society, nor the intellectuality of Plato's. To designate a model of the good society as the one which, if realized, would be morally best thus requires a choice among competing values.

Appreciation of how choice among values enters into the endorsement of social ideals leads easily to despair about whether agreement on the nature of the good society can be reached. Since the choice of values on which such agreement rests is ineluctably contestable, it may seem hopeless to expect consensus concerning which model of the good society is best. Why should any advocate change his choice, when it rests as much as all the others on an incorrigible moral preference? And if the basis for designating any model of the good society as morally best is incorrigible, arguments for or against so designating anarchy are pointless. Once beliefs about the nature of the good society are seen to be contestable, it may seem that the task of evaluating an ideal anarchy must be abandoned.

This conclusion should be resisted, since the value of a social ideal depends significantly on considerations which have nothing to do with moral preference. One of those considerations is attainability. A model of a good society with patently unattainable characteristics, such as costless methods of production or telepathic minds, is ineligible for the status of morally best, because it gives bad practical advice. By calling on us to work for advantages that cannot possibly be won, it directs activity into a path that must be fruitless. Another way of showing why unattainable models of the good society lack moral value is to consider what would happen if they had it. The way would then be open for the most inventive dreamer to claim, validly, that since he had equipped his model with the greatest number of good though unattainable features, it deserved designation as morally best.

If anarchy is, as some have claimed, a condition plainly beyond reach, it is no more eligible for selection as the best regime than any other unachievable social system. There are two main arguments for calling anarchy unreachable. One denies the slightest possibility of success for the strategy that must prepare the way for it. The other, focusing on anarchy as a finished structure, views its achievement as precluded by incompatibilities among its elements. Ample evidence has been assembled in this book to meet these arguments.

The prospects for anarchist strategy have certainly been revealed in the course of this analysis as slight. The dilemma in which anarchists are caught by their need to produce sweeping changes without deceit or force has thus far prevented all of their strategies from being effective. Yet past failure to devise measures that can set the stage for anarchy is not proof that such measures lie beyond reach forever. One or more of the conditions that have for so long stymied anarchist endeavor might some day relent. Nor can one entirely dismiss the promise of creative innovation. Anarchy would be disqualified for consideration as the ideally best social order only if the strategy needed to attain it faced permanent defeat. But even after fullest weight has been given to its historic failure, the possibility that anarchist strategy will be successful remains. The argument that strategic unattainability excludes anarchy from consideration as the ideally best regime must therefore be rejected as unpersuasive.

Though a strategy that prepares for anarchy must be accounted possible, anarchy would still not qualify as a model of the good society if the main attributes of its completed structure could not coexist. Points of friction among these attributes are numerous. The rich diversity that marks anarchist society is supposed to be accompanied by equality of status. Yet the normal tendency of people to evaluate each other means that differences of kind encourage differences of rank. The censure which is anarchy's distinctive method of control is supposed to occur among persons who are open and forthright. Yet the threat of rebuke, which anarchist censure poses, prompts all but the bravest to hide from surveillance by being secretive. But of the many points of friction which trouble a complete anarchy, the most dangerous to its integrity is the friction, previously analyzed in detail, between its members' individuality and their communal ties. Anarchist individuality and community are patently discordant. Individuality, especially if conceived in Kropotkin's way as creative uniqueness, but also if conceived generically, as rational independence, is a trait that renders the self separate. Developed individuals, in all their anarchist delineations, tend to become detached by virtue of their self-assertion from their fellow humans. Just as individuality fragments community, so community makes it hard for individuality to grow. The reciprocal awareness which constitutes the communal bond of anarchy is a significantly repressive force, which, through pressures toward conformity, saps personal independence. If anarchy is not to be pre-emptorily disqualified as a possible model of the good society, it must be shown to be attainable despite its internal frictions.

One of the arguments sometimes used to show the inner harmony of anarchy is lame and facile. Anarchy, according to this argument, has remarkably accordant attributes. They only appear at odds because they are illegitimately viewed as having to exist under the state's inhospitable conditions. Diversity will of course undermine equality wherever the state, through its impersonality, renders its subjects envious and grasping. Censure will of course discourage openness and honesty wherever subjects have to hide their selves from the state's remote presence. Individuality and community will of course be enemies where there is a state to homogenize subjects and cut off the wellsprings of reciprocal awareness at their individual source. But since the state-imposed conditions which render the attributes of anarchy incompatible are absent from the setting in which complete anarchy occurs, the claim that anarchy's internal incompatibilities make it un-attainable must be rejected as resting on a contextual mistake.

The weakness of this argument lies in its assumption that the sufficient condition for rendering the attributes of anarchy compatible is statelessness. Even though the state's presence is an obvious source of the conflicts among the attributes of anarchy, these conflicts may plausibly be suspected of being overdetermined by a team of cooperating causes. To vindicate their social ideal as harmonious enough to be achievable, anarchists must therefore do more than trace its internal incompatibilities to the state's effects; they must also show that in a stateless condition these incompatibilities would not arise from other causes. Anarchist theory contains material to demonstrate this point.

Anarchists show an appreciation, with which they are too seldom credited, for the insufficiency of mere statelessness as a setting for their system. Statelessness must in their view be preceded and accompanied by conditions which combat the numerous causes of anarchy's internal friction that statelessness cannot defeat alone. When legal government and social hierarchy have completed their civilizing missions, when economic advances have ended the need for abject poverty and for the most servile industrial routines, when anarchist endeavor has weakened the destructive tendencies of habit, fear and envy, and has strengthened more cooperative, sympathetic, reasonable dispositions, then and only then will statelessness, now operating in a context which dampens anarchy's internal frictions, be a source of harmony. If the anarchists claimed that statelessness alone resolved such conflicts in their social model as those between diversity and equality, censure and honesty, or individuality and community, then anarchy would have to be judged too discordant to qualify for consideration as the best regime. But since statelessness is but one of the forces on which anarchists rely to give harmony to their system, and since their various remedies for discord, taken together, are not obviously ineffective, anarchy remains eligible, despite its internal conflicts, for designation as the ideal social order.

The case for acknowledging anarchy as attainable, despite its internal discords, rests on more than the impossibility of altogether denying its capacity to form a coherent structure. Besides offering this minimal defense of their model's inner unity, anarchists also deploy a bolder argument. Since no complete anarchy has ever been established, the compatibility of its attributes cannot be tested by direct experience. But the question of their compatibility is not entirely beyond indirect empirical assessment. Numerous social arrangements which resemble anarchy harmoniously combine attributes whose compatibility in a state of anarchy is suspect. We have already encountered some of these arrangements, when we examined the circles of conversers, producers and neighbors used by the various anarchists to exemplify their society's structure. Kropotkin, in his descriptions of primitive societies, village communes, medieval cities and contemporary organizations for voluntary aid, such as the English Life-Boat Association, furnishes additional examples of harmonious relations in settings that resemble anarchy.[1] In all of these settings individuality and community, to take only anarchy's most troublingly discordant attributes, not only coexist, but give each other varying degrees of mutual support. In the Life-Boat Association, for example, which consists of volunteers who save shipwrecked survivors, reciprocal awareness of pursuing a daring purpose strengthens each member's independent resolve, while the adroitness and determination of the individual members strengthens the ties of community which unite them. Anarchy is, of course, so much more complex, encompassing and stateless than these quasi-anarchist arrangements that their success in reconciling anarchy's discordant elements is no proof that anarchy can reconcile them. But their ability to do so makes the coherence of anarchy plausible enough so that qualms about its qualifications as an ideal social model which arise from concern about its internal frictions must be cast off as unreasonable.

The merit of a completed anarchy, now eligible for consideration by virtue of its having been proved attainable, turns on the balance between its morally objectionable and its morally valuable features. No definitive striking of this balance, which may well be impossible to achieve, will be attempted here. What will be offered are remarks aimed at highlighting the moral deficiencies and attractions of the anarchist ideal. These remarks, though inconclusive, will dispel misconceptions about anarchy's worth and open the way to more clearly appreciating its merit as a social model.

It must be recognized, to begin with, that anarchy suffers from neither of two moral shortcomings which are frequently ascribed to it. Its members exhibit none of that socially destructive selfishness which led Edward Hyndman to denounce it as 'individualism gone wild'. Nor are its members smothered in oppressive peer group pressures, such as have prompted a recent commentator to liken anarchy to 'an adolescent gang'.[2] Our understanding of how individuality and community are reinforcing under anarchy compels us to acknowledge its freedom from these defects. Neither a shattering individualism nor a stifling communitarianism contaminates an ideal anarchy, because its individualizing and communalizing tendencies fructify each other so as to prevent destructive excess.

Anarchy does, of course, have genuine defects, but some are not particularly objectionable or severe. These include its incomplete provision for privacy, for emotional self-expression and for meeting claims of distributive justice.

The opportunity to act and think without surveillance by unchosen others which we call privacy is greater in some models of the good society (such as J. S. Mill's), and perhaps even in some actual societies, than under anarchy. As was discovered when examining Godwin's conversational anarchy, its members are unable, except by retreating into solitude and by counting on their interlocutors' discretion, to escape being observed. In the more complex societies of the later anarchists opportunities for privacy are no doubt greater. But anarchy in all its variants remains a system where privacy, since it involves social indifference and personal concealment, is hardly salient.

To appreciate how far anarchy is morally deficient for limiting privacy, one must bear in mind the conditions which, in a state of anarchy, cause the need for privacy to diminish. Privacy fills two quite different needs: it is both a refuge from incursions by the malevolent or insensitive and a place of seclusion for inner growth or restoration. Now the members of an anarchy, owing to their mutual awareness, their honest sympathy and their commitment to controlling behavior with reasons, are neither the sanctimonious Pecksniffs, nor the barefaced prigs, and certainly not the domineering zealots against whom the refuge of privacy is urgent. As for privacy as seclusion, there is no reason to doubt that under anarchy it is available. Certainly Godwin, who devotes much attention to this subject, praises solitude. And anarchist individuals have a discrete sensitivity to their neighbors' moods. Since seclusion, which is the type of privacy needed in an anarchy, is the type that anarchy provides, its lack of the privacy that serves as a refuge is not a defect to regard as grave.

No less marked than anarchy's deficiency as a provider of privacy is its deficiency as a setting for emotional self-expression. Its shortcomings as a facilitator of emotions must not be exaggerated. Even Godwin, for whom feelings are no part of individuality, grants that they contribute to its growth. Expressions of emotion are therefore by no means absent from Godwinian anarchy, but being ancillary to its nature, they have an insecure presence. The later anarchists, by endowing their conceptions of individuality with emotional attributes, give feelings in their good society a safer place. In Kropotkin's anarchy, the display of emotions remains limited, because reasoned argument – which Kropotkin, following earlier anarchists, makes the first defense against misconduct – is jeopardized not only by displays of destructive feelings such as selfishness, fear or envy, which in an anarchy would diminish, but also by the display of less harmful and more permanent emotions. Alarm, triumph, despair, impatience, indeed almost the whole gamut of human feelings, though surely they would continue to be experienced under anarchy, would sometimes have to be repressed. Their frequent expression would certainly be normal, but since not even the influence of a full-fledged anarchy can entirely prevent emotional outbursts from disrupting the practice of controlling behavior with reasoned arguments, or the process of rational deliberation on which this practice rests, the unlimited display of feelings in an anarchy is unallowable. What thus emerges at the root of anarchy's deficiency as a setting for emotional self-expression is its remarkably tenacious devotion to sovereign reason.

Whether the rationality that anarchy provides is worth the price of a somewhat limited emotional self-expression is a question which will be addressed later in this chapter. The point that now needs making is that anarchy, in order to achieve utmost communal individuality and freedom, must pay this price. It remained for those recent sympathizers with anarchism who have been most touched by disillusionment with rationality to give up the conviction of anarchy's devisers that reliance on the giving of reasons is the wellspring of its moral worth. Believing the old anarchists to have been too optimistic in their estimates of human reasonableness, finding emotional attributes of the self more at the center of individuality than rational attributes, and having witnessed too much use of reason for evil ends to trust the reasoner any longer, a motley assortment of contemporary writers and activists claims to have devised a new form of anarchy in which the avowedly non-rational display of emotions, especially by evanescent leaders performing spectacular gestures, replaces reason as the chief regulating force.[3] The society envisaged by this group of authors, being stateless, and directed toward attaining communal individuality, can certainly be called a type of anarchy. But it is an anarchy with less of the freedom that is one of classical anarchy's chief attractions. The remarkable amount of freedom in the anarchy studied in this book arises from a marked absence of hindrances, including emotional hindrances, to deliberation, choice and conduct. Proceeding from the scarcely deniable premise according to which freedom is undiminished by the rationally based conclusions which a deliberating agent reaches about the merit of his contemplated acts, the founders of anarchism devised a model of the good society which protects these conclusions, and hence freedom, from every sort of threat. There must be less freedom in the model of the good society devised by recent non-rational anarchists, because it includes emotional displays which jeopardize the rationally based conclusions on which freedom in an anarchy must rest. The extensive freedom of classical anarchy is simply unobtainable without the limits on emotional self-expression that non-rational anarchists reject.

The partial shortcoming of anarchy that remains to be considered is its slighting in its pattern of economic distribution of some established claims of justice. The anarchists, we have discovered, increasingly choose need over productive contribution as the distributive claim the good society must meet. This choice, despite its certain merit, has the drawback of denying recognition to other worthy claims. Members of an anarchy with extraordinary talents or abilities receive less material advantage than other ideal societies provide them, and, under conditions of scarcity, not enough to exploit their endowments fully. Nor are benefits bestowed to the same extent as in some other ideal societies on persons who show unusual diligence or daring. Because anarchy is so devoted to satisfying the claim of need, it must neglect these rival claims of justice.

The moral defect incurred by anarchy from this neglect is mitigated by how it organizes production and by how its members view productive work. One good reason for honoring claims of contribution, ability or effort is to increase well-being (perhaps above all of the least favored) through eliciting plentiful and efficient production. The prospect of receiving economic benefit for adding to the supply of goods, for exercising natural talents and for hard or dangerous work is normally a stimulus to productivity. Viewed from this angle, the merit of claims to remuneration that rival that of need lies not in their intrinsic fittingness but in their utility as incentives. Now conditions in an ideal anarchy are such that bounteous, efficient production occurs without these incentives. The mutual understanding among participants in anarchy, their desire to develop their native talents, the satisfaction they find in their often voluntary, varied work, and their ability, owing to polytechnical education and occupational mobility, to understand the productive process as a whole, are some of the reasons why it is unnecessary in an anarchy to distribute economic benefits according to claims of contribution, ability or effort. One can nevertheless argue plausibly that though conditions under anarchy assure ample productivity, even if these claims are slighted, they should be honored anyway, as claims to just desert. The claim that seems most to deserve recognition on this basis is (conscientious) effort. That producers who are especially brave or diligent should be rewarded economically, whether or not rewarding them is generally advantageous, is an intuitively appealing proposition, which serves as a defensible ground for deeming anarchy's neglect of effort in its pattern of distribution to be a real, though far from overwhelming, moral defect.

If its incomplete recognition of privacy, emotional self-expression and the claims of distributive justice were anarchy's only shortcomings, there would probably be wide agreement that it is the model of the good society which, if realized, would be morally best. But anarchy also suffers from a fourth deficiency, which is complete and more open to objection. This is its repudiation of active citizenship. A vision of the citizen as an equal participant in the process of self-government is a recurrent theme in political theory, most eloquently articulated in modern times by Rousseau. The citizens of Rousseau's direct democracy, who subordinate their personal interests to the good of the whole, who eschew the distractions of activity in partial groups, and whose chief business is to deliberate and vote on laws, are figures who, despite their awesome virtues, have no place in a mature anarchy. We have already discovered, in examining the anarchists' criticism of unanimous direct democracy, that a main reason they object to such a government is for its homogenizing public spirit. Participants in a unanimous direct democracy view legislative proposals with an aloof disinterest that anarchists reject for being repugnant to developed individuality. Now the homogenizing public spirit which anarchists reject in a unanimous direct democracy, far from being peculiar to that bizarre form of government, must be a part of any which includes an active citizenry. For unless citizens who participate in the legislative process as equals subordinate their particular concerns to the general good, the laws they enact will be so shortsighted and divisive that social peace will be endangered. According to the anarchists, then, active citizenship, in all its forms, though not without attractions, still must be excluded from their model of the good society as injurious to the independent, particularized sort of individual that it is a main purpose of that society to promote.

It might be thought that the exclusion by the anarchists of active citizenship from any place in their good society rests on a mistaken understanding of its relationship to individuality. If being an individual and being a citizen were compatible, then anarchy, contrary to the belief of its espousers, could enjoy the benefits of both.

One of the best reasons for accepting the anarchists' view of citizenship at odds with individuality is its acceptance by citizenship's proponents. Rousseau, for instance, acknowledges that in his society of equal citizens individuality must be repressed. The individual man 'is the unit, the whole, dependent only on himself'. Man as citizen 'is but the numerator of a fraction, whose value depends on the denominator; . . .he no longer regards himself as one, but as part of the whole, and is only conscious of the common life'. Since individuality subverts commitment to the public, 'you must take your choice between man and the citizen, you cannot train both'.[4] The contradiction between man as individual and as citizen, which Rousseau drew so starkly, has remained a chief preoccupation of political theorists who admire active citizenship. Most have tried through some means such as pluralism or functional representation to reduce the force of the contradiction, but none have denied that it exists. Michael Walzer, for instance, ends his anguished discussion of citizenship with a plea for kibitzers, not so much because he finds them likeable as because they narrow the inevitable gap between 'the world of the meeting' and the world of 'the tête-à-tête'.[5] Since proponents of citizenship would surely embrace full individual development, if they thought it was safe, their refusal to do so is strong evidence of its incompatibility with citizenship and hence that the defect anarchy suffers owing to its lack of citizens is beyond escape.

Anarchy's repudiation of active citizenship is more serious than its other shortcomings, not only because it is total, whereas they are partial, but also because it is more morally offensive. The ideal of the self-governing citizen has legitimate appeal. Man the citizen, who obeys his own laws, is one version of man at his very best: self-directing, public spirited, controlling his own destiny. That anarchy is seriously deficient for excluding citizens is a conclusion that only those who find citizenship worthless can reject.

Yet in an anarchist society the lack of citizens is less disturbing than it is in other societies, because the communal individuality prevailing in an anarchy affords one of the chief advantages of citizenship. Rousseau condemned existing society as strongly as the anarchists, and for similar reasons. Both saw it as composed of competitive, self-centered role-players, utterly bereft of mutual understanding. Citizenship was Rousseau's hope for ending this estrangement and for providing a more communal existence. Centering their lives around deliberation in the public forum, where each gives his disinterested opinion on proposed legislation and is respectfully attended to by all the rest, Rousseauist citizens develop a strong mutual awareness. They do lack individuality, but this is the price they pay for their community. It is because they are so limited as particular individuals that the communal bond among these deliberating citizens is intense.

Anarchists, of course, are as determined as Rousseau to create community where now there is estrangement. But whereas Rousseau, because he confined community to life in the forum, suppressed individuality as a disruptive influence, the anarchists, because they suffuse community through all of life, welcome individuality as a cohesive force. Personal particularity and independence, instead of dividing the members of an anarchy, make them more apt for their variegated communal existence. By increasing their appeal for one another, and their dependence on one another for the satisfaction of needs, individuality intensifies their mutual awareness. It is thus because anarchy provides community even though it lacks citizens that the offensiveness of this lack is lessened. But it nevertheless remains a moral defect.

For even though the absence of citizens does not deprive anarchy of community, it does deprive it of a source of noble eminence.

To reach a verdict on whether anarchy is the ideal social order its assets as well as its shortcomings need assessment. One of its chief assets, the conjoint provision of ample individuality and community, certainly has great merit, though hardly enough to make anarchy's status as the best regime uncontroversial. What is most crucial to assessing the moral worth of anarchy is its problematic exaltation of a freedom that is rationally based.

No one in the history of political theory has advanced a more exigent concept of freedom than the anarchists, because none has required that agents, to count as free, be as unhindered by restraints. For anarchists, it will be recalled, a completely free agent is liberated in both action and choice from every removable hindrance, except for those arising from his rational deliberation. If the anarchists said no more about the restraints that count as non-coercive than that they are rationally based, their concept of liberty would not be particularly exigent. Many political theorists who are far from being libertarians have conceived of freedom as a matter of rational control. What gives the freedom of the anarchists its special exigence is their insistence that the deliberative process whose conclusions are non-coercive must be rational in a more than minimal sense. This process must be rational in the sense of systematic and critical, to be sure. In weighing the arguments and evidence which bear on whether to perform an act, the deliberating agent must use standards which he has judged acceptable by methodical examination and which he applies consistently to his relevantly similar conduct. But deliberation, for anarchists, must be rational in a stronger sense than this in order for its conclusions to be coercionless. It must be thoroughly particular in having for its focus the advantages and disadvantages attached to the performance of a single act. If, after deliberating, I choose to do an act because it is of a type whose general performance I believe to have good consequences, or because it is enjoined by a rule I deem inviolable, or because some person or organization whose judgment I respect prescribes it, anarchists regard my deliberation as non-rational. For I have failed to consider the particular circumstances of the case. The only deliberation that is rational enough to make me free involves attending to all the concrete details that bear on my act's merit, and especially to the consequences for the particular individuals who would be touched by its effects.[6] Even in an anarchy, where access to such details is easy, such particularized deliberation is hard, relentless work. It is the dependence of anarchist freedom on such a demanding rationality that raises questions about the value of its contribution to anarchy's moral worth.

Doubts concerning the value of anarchist freedom are bound to grow more urgent when one appreciates that the rationality on which it depends is purely procedural. It specifies only the manner in which the members of an anarchy must choose their acts and says nothing about the attributes their acts must have. I act rationally, in an anarchy, no matter what I do, just so long as systematic, critical, particularized deliberation is the means I use to choose my conduct. The anarchist view of rationality as a matter of nothing but procedure calls the worth of the freedom which depends on it into question by making that freedom consistent with performing abominable acts. The only restraints that do not curtail anarchist freedom are imposed by the conclusions drawn by individuals from their rational deliberations. Since the rationality of these deliberations is procedural, they can warrant any act. Freedom in an anarchy, owing to its dependence on a procedural rationality, thus serves as a license for misconduct. How can anarchy possibly be the ideal social model, when its freedom, besides demanding burdensome particularized deliberation, allows wrong-doing? To make the case for anarchy as the best regime in face of the stiff price in laborious deliberation and in opportunities to misbehave that its rationally demanding, behaviorally permissive freedom exacts, what must be shown is that, despite these drawbacks, anarchy is imbued by its freedom with sufficient value to tip the moral balance in its favor.

One benefit of anarchist freedom that must not be overlooked in an overall assessment of its value is its service to communal individuality. The anarchists, we have discovered, prize freedom mainly as a support for the communal individuality that is their chief objective. It is largely by stripping away the hindrances to choice and conduct, except for those which are rationally based, that anarchists encourage mutual awareness and self-development. Intellectual independence and forthright communication are leading attributes of their goal that anarchists expect an atmosphere of their kind of liberty to nurture. The service anarchist freedom renders to communal individuality surely helps offset its moral drawbacks.

The limit anarchists place on the scope of liberty adds to its moral value by restricting how far it licenses wrongful acts. Freedom in an anarchy, though remarkably extensive, nevertheless is incomplete, because decisions and conduct governed by the agent's rationally based conclusions sometimes are impeded. The frailty of reasoned argument does not escape the anarchists, who enlist internalization, positional authority and censorial rebuke as supplementary means of regulation. If an act, though rationally based, would cause serious harm, coercion from one or more of these three sources deprives participants in anarchy of the freedom to choose or do it. It is true that those who apply this coercion do so on the basis of a deliberative rationality that is just as procedural as that of the agent whose freedom they curtail. Being no more equipped than he is with standards for judging the attributes of conduct, they enjoy an equally generous license for misbehavior and relieve the agent of his objectionably permissive freedom through using an objectionably permissive freedom of their own. Hence the limit anarchists place on the scope of liberty certainly does not rid it of moral license, for while it somewhat diminishes opportunities for misconduct, it leaves substantial freedom to misbehave.

Though the dependence of anarchist freedom on procedural rationality renders it distressingly permissive, making it depend on substantive rationality, so as to cure this defect, would bring another, which, from the anarchist perspective, is worse. Anarchists prize their freedom because its liberation of action and choice from every hindrance except for those which the agent himself deems right helps communal individuality to grow. Now substantive rationality differs from procedural by identifying acts which one might deem right as having attributes which make choosing or doing them non-rational. A freedom dependent on substantive rationality thus allows more interference with choice and action than a freedom dependent on procedural rationality does. Being more restrictive, it is less conducive than a freedom dependent on procedural rationality to the realization of the anarchists' final goal.

Remaining doubts about the merit of the anarchists' choice, as a chief attribute of the good society, of such a rationally demanding, behaviorally permissive freedom can be allayed, though not eliminated, by considering the conditions serving as a background where this freedom is enjoyed. It is unlikely that the members of an anarchy, even though they have freedom to cause harm, actually will cause it, because they deliberate under conditions which discourage them from choosing harmful acts. The equality of power, prestige and wealth among the members of an anarchy, as well as their close interdependence, tend to put harming others at odds with interest. The sincerity, respect, or benevolence that is anarchy's dominant social attitude tends to put such harm at odds with inclination. Conditions in an anarchy thus provide a context in which the exercise of freedom based on procedural rationality is rather safe.[7]

More might be said about why anarchist freedom is less objectionable than appears at first glance, but there is no denying that it suffers from grave defects. Even some who accurately appreciate its virtues, and who avoid exaggerating its faults, will legitimately deem the exigency and permissiveness of the freedom sought by anarchists inordinate enough to make their model of the good society unfit for the status of the best regime. But those of us who, in our reflective moments, exalt the personal particularity of the deliberation on which anarchist freedom rests, and who find its dependence on a substantively unlimited rationality inspiring, will hardly be considered outlandish if we advance the thesis that of all the ideal social models anarchy is the best. Every model of the good society has drawbacks, and anarchy, especially owing to its denial of a place to citizens, certainly has its share. But anarchy is also well endowed with assets. Its remarkable merger of individuality and communality through a substantively unlimited, particularized rationality makes it the setting for an illustrious way of life.

ANARCHY AS A CRITICAL STANDARD AND PRACTICAL GUIDE

To vindicate the choice of anarchy as the ideal social order, more must be considered than its merit once achieved. Though a state of perfect anarchy cannot be deemed unreachable, the chance of reaching it must be accounted slight. The unlikelihood of attaining anarchy would diminish its value markedly, if its value resided only in its completed structure, for the value of a good lessens as the probability of achieving it declines. There is, however, hope of vindicating anarchy as the ideal social order, despite its unlikelihood as a complete achievement, because it also draws its value from another source. Anarchy serves not only as a model for a completely new society, but also as a standard for judging present society, and as a guide for moving from old to new. Since the value of anarchy as standard and guide is separate from its value as a finished model, even though this model will probably never be realized, anarchy may still be the good society with the greatest moral worth.

There is a well-known and persistent objection to the value as standard and guide of an ideal like anarchy, which is exigent, improbable, and morally appealing. Such an ideal is viewed by many as singularly dangerous on the ground that its practical use causes grave, uncompensated harm. Being dramatically different from the established social order, an ideal like anarchy calls on those who rely on it for guidance to take steps which, since they include substantial suffering, coercion and deceit, are both inherently reprehensible and in moral conflict with the ideal for whose sake they are carried out. The harm caused by these measures might be justified, if they realized the ideal toward which they point, because the moral excellence of that ideal might be great enough to outweigh all harm caused by the steps needed to achieve it. What makes the practical use of the ideal abhorrent, according to this argument, is the improbability of its attainment.

Since the ideal, being unlikely to be realized, will almost certainly not yield the benefits for whose sake it calls for harm, its practical use is cruel and reckless. An exigent, improbable social ideal, even though, like anarchy, it is morally appealing, must be rejected as a critical standard and practical guide as a self-defeating source of evil.[8]

This abstract argument against ideals which are exigent, improbable and appealing is most tellingly applied to the ideal sought during the Russian Revolution. The spectacle of Marx's vision of the good society being debased by terror and repression as its admirers struggled vainly to achieve it leads understandably to the view that exigent, improbable, appealing ideals should always be renounced. That this conclusion follows even in the Russian case is doubtful, since devotion to their ideal may not have been the reason why the Russian revolutionaries caused such hardship. Adverse circumstances or a misreading by the revolutionaries of their ideal's practical significance are equally plausible explanations. But however strong this argument may be against other social ideals, that of the anarchists has attributes which greatly blunt its force. The forthright rationality, personal independence and communal solidarity that characterize a complete anarchy constrain efforts to achieve it so as to make them benign. It is because the anarchists appreciate how the development of these characteristics depends on what happens during the preparatory period that they require favorable attitudes and circumstances to prevail before struggle for their good society begins, that they minimize the place of coercion and fraud in the waging of this struggle, and that they insist on advancing mainly through the force of argument and example. All of these constraints on anarchist practice protect those who engage in it from causing uncompensated harm, by helping to prevent them from inflicting the inordinate suffering that so often accompanies untrammeled struggle. Thus the ideal of anarchy, because it constrains efforts to rebuild society so as to protect them from excess, though exigent, improbable and morally appealing, promises to serve practice safely.

Those whom history has taught to fear bold ideals may still

suspect that the limits which anarchy places on efforts designed
to reach it, and which promise to make these efforts safe, are all
too likely to be abandoned in the heat of struggle. 'The spirit of
revolt', which energizes anarchist endeavor for Kropotkin, has an
equivalent for his predecessors. All of the anarchists envision
workers for their ideal as enthusiastic, bold and steadfast. The
ideal they are seeking, while not unquestionably beyond their
grasp, is not likely to be reached. Would it be surprising if these
devoted workers, troubled by frustration, impatience and despair,
betrayed their ideal by renouncing the limits it sets on practice as
intolerable? No matter that this betrayal makes their ideal per-
manently unreachable. In the heat of struggle, energy is concen-
trated on immediate efforts, and fine perceptions about future
consequences are lost.

Examples which might be read as accrediting this scenario can
be found in the history of Spanish anarchism. Part of what
incited the anarchist *pistoleros* during the civil war to execute
summarily so many innocents may have been a response to the
difficulty of realizing an exigent ideal. Astounded by the difference between their own society and the one they sought, dis-
heartened by setbacks, and overwhelmed by the obstacles their
project faced, the *pistoleros* may have succumbed to the desperate
hope, tempting to anyone in their plight, that in a sufficiently
convulsive upheaval their ideal would prevail miraculously. Here,
as in the case of the Russian Revolution, blaming the harm
caused by attempts to reconstruct society on the boldness of the
ideal being sought is speculative and conjectural. Numerous other
plausible explanations, ranging from fascination with the cult of
death to the imperatives of total war, have been offered for the
Spanish anarchists' excesses. To hold the exigency and improbability of their ideal responsible for the uncompensated damage
caused by their attempts to rebuild society is thus out of the
question. Nevertheless, taken as a warning, the abstract argument
against using exigent ideals for guidance retains some point; for it
has to be admitted that pursuing such an ideal, even when, like
anarchy, it carries limits, risks causing damage that would not
occur if the ideal had been renounced.

Before accepting the argument for renunciation, one needs to recognize that acting without the guidance of exigent ideals also carries risks. There are various conclusions concerning political activity that someone who refuses to be guided by exigent ideals might reach. He might become complacent, believing all reformative endeavor dangerous; he might use his renunciation as an excuse for indolence, for refraining from efforts to improve society while continuing to denounce it as reprehensible; or he might opt for a cautious incrementalism. The first two conclusions can be summarily dismissed for condoning blatant suffering. Incrementalism, which can alleviate existing misery, needs closer consideration as a guide to action free of the dangers that bedevil exigence.

The incrementalist is like the complacent and indolent renouncers of bold ideals in accepting the established social system as a whole. Where he differs is in striving to improve the existing system through cautious modification and reforms. Meliorative activity that proceeds through small, predictable, reversible adjustments, and that has the lessening of felt misery as its aim, he supports fervently. What the incrementalist opposes are efforts, which the use of exigent ideals as guides suggests, aimed at increasing future welfare through replacing the established social system with an entirely new one. Such efforts are denounced by the incrementalist, for reasons just examined, as dangerous sources of uncompensated suffering; but he is moved by his appreciation of how the established system causes misery to proceed gradually, without the help of an ideal social model, toward ridding it of the traits widely perceived as most harmful.[9]

While incrementalism must surely be preferred to complacency or indolence as a guide to action, it is not obviously preferable to an ideal like anarchy, which, though exigent, hedges action in its service with constraints. For incrementalism, because it eschews reference to exigent ideals, ignores or tolerates objectionable features of established social systems which practice guided by such ideals contests. Any exigent social model identifies underlying sources of misery in the existing society which may not elicit much alarm, and which, being inherent in its nature, cannot be eliminated unless the whole society is replaced. The anarchist social model, to take the exigent ideal with which we are now fully acquainted, identifies inherent features of modern society, such as law and hierarchy, as the taproots of its members' stunted, estranged existence. The incrementalist, because he accepts the existing social system and tries to improve it only by diminishing its most immediate sources of felt misery, leaves undisturbed the inherent, underlying evils to which an exigent ideal like anarchy calls attention. Thus, though incrementalism offers comforting protection against fanatical excess, its repudiation of ideals as guides to action is a burdensome source of dread. For incrementalists are condemned to live with the daily apprehension that promising opportunities to augment human welfare are being missed.

Even though incrementalism leaves possibilities for human welfare unfulfilled, as a practical guide it is still preferable to social ideals whose unlimited exigence makes using them for guidance likely to wreak serious uncompensated harm. But anarchy, we have discovered, owing to the constraints it puts on efforts to rebuild society, is an ideal which can be pursued without much risk of havoc. That those who seek anarchy will ignore the constraints it sets on action is of course a remote danger, but one worth accepting, if its practical guidance leads to appreciably greater benefits than can be secured through incrementalism. The practical value of anarchy thus depends not only, or even mainly, on the danger of using it for guidance, but also on how much advantage its use as a guide can bring.

The first practical use to which an ideal like anarchy can be fruitfully put is as a standard for judging an established social system. Anarchy, when used to judge modern industrial society, raises deep objections to many of its most generally accepted traits. Rather than rehearsing all of these objections, it should suffice at this stage of analysis to recall the most distinctive – those directed against legality. Judged against the standard of an ideal anarchy, modern society appears seriously defective for controlling behavior by means of law, whose generality, permanence and physical coercion make it impossible for community or individuality to develop fully, let alone to merge. The practical effect of using anarchy as a critical standard is thus to make law (along with several other essential attributes of existing society) the target of relentless attack.

The animus which anarchy, used as a standard, directs against the rule of law is expressed not just in hostile declarations, but also more creatively in concrete criticism. The founders of anarchism, starting with Godwin, all marshalled evidence, drawn from history and their own experience, of how law serves those who are ascendent to keep their inferiors in tow, of how its permanence and generality cause crude, misguided behavioral regulation, and of how the predictability, which is law's redeeming asset, remains in fact a will-o'-the-wisp. Though law promises to bring certainty, what it actually amounts to, says Godwin, is 'a labyrinth without end, . . .a mass of contradictions that cannot be untangled'.[10] This genre of concrete criticism of legal institutions, inaugurated by the founders, has been much elaborated in recent times by empirically oriented observers who have studied law from the anarchists' critical perspective. Lester Mazor, for example, ascribes the numerous cases of legal oppression, ineptitude and caprice that he has collected in his essay on 'Disrespect for Law' to 'the limits of rules as means of accomplishing change and as an expression of the character of social relations'.[11] The concrete criticism of established institutions, which arises from judging them against the anarchist ideal, gives more impetus to efforts to rebuild society than criticism which, however vigorous, remains abstract. For outrage against an abstraction like legality gains strength and focus when the abstraction is seen as causing specific evils. But if the anarchist ideal served practically as no more than a critical standard, it could not easily be proved more beneficial in its bearing on efforts to rebuild society than incrementalism. Concrete criticism, by itself, has diagnostic value, but it is more likely to yield advantage if accompanied by a plan of action. Fortunately, anarchy, in its practical use, serves not only as a standard for judging the ills of established society, but also as a guide to their cure. It is the guidance anarchy gives to social reconstruction that is most crucial for assessing its value as applied to practice.

The safety which the founders imparted to anarchist struggles by hedging them with constraints is somewhat unreliable, chiefly because these struggles have as their strategic aim to substitute full-fledged anarchy for the industrialized nation-state. The founding anarchists justified the actions they recommended as the most likely, among those falling within permissible limits, to achieve this substitution. So long as anarchists decide what to do by reference to the effectiveness of their efforts for replacing the modern state, they will be tempted to disregard the constraints which limit their activity and promise to make it safe. To replace the modern state with a full-fledged anarchy is so difficult that anarchists for whom this is the chief practical concern must find the conditions, scruples and timetables that constrain their efforts hard to support. The obvious way to give action guided by the anarchist ideal the safety it needs to be more beneficial than action guided by incrementalism is to set the strategic aim of replacing the nation-state by anarchy aside. For when this replacement ceases to be the anarchist's main concern, he will be less prone to view the constraints his ideal sets on practice as fetters.

There are other reasons, besides safety, for giving up the strategic aim of replacing the state with anarchy. For one thing, this move, while not made explicitly by any founder, was certainly suggested by some of them. Godwin, in his view of progress toward rationality as unending, and Proudhon, in his plea for withdrawal by anarchists into their own separate organizations, both implied that the main concern in deciding on present action should not be whether the contemplated course will best serve to replace the state with anarchy. Many of the most thoughtful recent anarchists, more despondent than their forebears about the prospects for destroying, dissolving or otherwise eliminating industrialized nation-states, let alone replacing them with anarchy, and more fearful of the unredeemed suffering to which attempts to do this might lead, have pursued in their writings, as well as in their activities, the founders' intimations about efforts directed at achieving something less than a fully anarchist society on the scale of existing states. These recent extensions of the anarchist tradition, designed to give it safe purchase on the present social world, have produced marked benefits. A brief sketch of how anarchists of late have been using their social model to guide partial anarchization within the nation-state is thus required before the practical value of the anarchist model can be assessed accurately.

A quotation from Karl Landauer, chosen by Colin Ward as the motto for *Anarchy*, his journal which, in the 1960s, championed partial anarchist endeavors, aptly captures their underlying inspiration. 'The state is a condition, a certain relationship between human beings, a mode of behavior; we destroy it by behaving differently.'[12] Anarchists who have approached action from Landauer's angle have carried out two types of changes, both of which achieve some measure of immediate anarchization. The first rearranges some particularly significant social activity, while leaving the structure of other activities undisturbed. The second rearranges all of the social activities occurring in a particular place, but makes no direct attempt to rearrange them elsewhere.

The first type of change is well illustrated by the accomplishments of anarchists concerned with education, who have used their ideal social model for guidance in establishing schools with as many features of a complete anarchy as can feasibly be incorporated into an organization like a school, which is not an independent social system. The Ferrer Modern School of New York, which functioned with many changes from 1911 to 1953, exemplifies how anarchists have derived benefits from using their model to guide the restructuring of education. 'Very young children' in the Modern School, as described by one of its organizers, learn 'nearly all the major parts of anthropology... through the desire that so many of them have to make things'. Education, as practiced in the Modern School, thus 'combines training of the senses and of the mind, skill of hand and skill of brain', just as they are combined in a complete anarchy. The Modern School also follows the anarchist model in its abhorrence of legality. 'We do away with all coercive discipline and all the rules and paraphernalia of such discipline: the raised desk of the teacher, the rigid rows of seats for the children, and the ideal that every class should be conducted according to. . .preconceived codes.' Finally, the Modern School draws from the ideal of anarchy its emphasis in the classroom on unrestrained discussion of 'problems suggested by the children, . . .which is of the very greatest aid in developing the children as separate, thinking individuals and as members of the social unit'.[13] The steps anarchists have been taking to restructure education have yielded advantages, without wreaking uncompensated harm of the sort that struggles to replace the state with anarchy threaten. At the very least, anarchist education has saved some children from the inflexible discipline common in our schools, which often teaches that learning is something to resent. More positively, anarchist education has surely, though to an unmeasurable extent, aided the growth of independent rationality and voluntary cooperation.

Another social activity that has benefited from being partially reorganized along lines indicated by the anarchist ideal is work. Anarchists who have been more concerned with restructuring productive activity within the state's jurisdiction so that it resembles what would occur under anarchy, than in using the workplace as a weapon in the struggle to replace the state, favor a self-management which, within the realm of the individual enterprise, is thoroughgoing. In the enterprises planned or established by these anarchists, internal decisions are made by neither owners, nor investors, nor managers, nor technicians, nor union officials, but consensually by all producers. The practice of self-management is ambiguous, because, depending on how far it goes, it has contrary effects. If producers make decisions on no matters except immediate conditions of work, the effect is often to increase efficiency, job satisfaction and profits. When self-management is extended upward to more significant matters – personnel, marketing, investment and the like – and when it is extended outward to decisions that affect the whole economy, the effect may be, though this is more speculative, to encourage producers, both in self-managed enterprises and in those with which they deal, to further restructure their activities along anarchist lines. The anarchists' recognition of this ambiguity in the practice of self-management is part of the reason why they require it to be thorough. But it is their determination to build as many features of an ideal anarchy into productive enterprises as is consistent with their remaining under the jurisdiction of the state that best explains not only the thoroughness of the self-management they advocate, but why it has distinctive features. In his essay on 'A Self-Employed Society' Colin Ward, working from the evidence of congenial, though non-anarchist examples, and of explicitly anarchist plans, describes the shape that an anarchist, though state-bound, self-management should take.[14] Voting and rule-making are de-emphasized in favor of open-ended discussion aiming toward consensus and the continuous process of 'one or two people thinking out and trying new things'. Consensual decisions are not enforced by designated supervisors, but by peers. There are no fixed roles; workers 'deploy themselves, depending on the requirements of the ongoing group task'. Finally, income is distributed equally among all members of the productive unit. Though enterprises organized like these are not intended, and could not be expected, to anarchize society completely, nevertheless, because they have so many anarchist features, they offer much of the advantage of a complete anarchy.

Besides restructuring particular activities on lines indicated by their social model, anarchists intent on immediate, though partial, progress also use their model to guide the reorganization of all activity within a circumscribed place, usually a farmland. Several rural settlements organized on anarchist principles were established in France at the beginning of this century, when the anarchist movement had been partially discredited by an epidemic of bomb-throwing and was threatened with being absorbed by syndicalism. Responding to this situation, a few French anarchists turned away from efforts to replace the state and founded an association whose purpose was to gather members, donations and sympathy so as to enable a site to be acquired for establishing an anarchist commune.

The story of the Colony of Vaux, founded by this association in 1903, parallels that of many similar endeavors. Having rented a house and about six acres of land on favorable terms from a friendly farmer, a half dozen settlers began living and working together according to certain arrangements. Before entering the commune, each agreed to do the necessary work and to renounce physical force. Necessities were taken, as needed, from communal stores, or, in case of shortage, distributed equally. Any productive surplus was also equally distributed. Collective decisions were made consensually, except for those concerning the admission of new members, which were made by unanimous vote. In case of strife that was 'a real danger to the general peace', offenders were 'invited' to leave. At first, the commune prospered, increasing in a few months to twenty-one members and successfully producing food and clothes. Despite the need to change their site, the colonists continued to live and work together for three years, after which disputes over alleged high-handedness by the leading founder caused them to disband.[15]

There are also numerous cases in the United States of anarchist settlements, starting in the mid-nineteenth century with Josiah Warren's experimental villages. One of the most ambitious and longest-lived of these settlements was the Ferrer Colony of Stelton, New Jersey, established in 1914 by the sponsors of the previously mentioned Modern School of New York. The Stelton Colony in its heyday in the 1920s had eighty or so families as permanent residents, as many as 100 boarding students in its elementary school, and an additional summer population of several hundred. It followed the usual anarchist pattern of unenforced consensual decision-making, and there was a great deal of shared cultural and educational activity, but in its economic arrangements it differed from the French settlements in that members owned their own houses and small plots of land, on which some farmed, while most commuted to work in New York City. Though plagued by growing controversy in the 1920s about whether to emphasize education or social action, and in the 1930s between those who remained anarchists and those who joined the Communist cause, the Stelton Colony, despite compromises both in its school and in its way of life, continued for over thirty years to offer many of the advantages of anarchy.[16]

Certain of the communes that were landmarks of the American

counter-culture in the 1960s have also been viewed, though less convincingly, as at least implicitly guided by the anarchist social model. The settlers of Cold Mountain Farm, which lasted barely through the summer of 1967, followed the advice of the impeccably anarchist Murray Bookchin. Yet many of them were moved more by yearnings for rustic simplicity or by oriental mysticism than by the intention to go as far as possible, on their small Vermont farm, toward building anarchy.[17] The very few Western communes which have been called anarchist by their founders or observers are even more remote in their inspiration from the anarchist ideal; and since some lasted longer than Cold Mountain, it can be shown that they diverge markedly from anarchy in their practice. Consider the case of Lou Gottlieb's Morningstar Ranch. Though anarchist in its avoidance of hierarchy, legality and physical coercion, Morningstar lacked the replacements for these practices which the ideal of anarchy suggests. Gottlieb, believing that 'the land selects the people', disliked collective decision making, no matter how consensual, resisted attempts to screen new settlers, and, in various ways, worked less for community than separation. No wonder that Morningstar was so beset by self-centered, destructive transients. Because, like most counter-culture communes which professed to follow the anarchist model, it tended to disregard that model's rational and solidaristic elements, it could achieve scarcely a semblance of the communal individuality to which a correct application of the anarchist model points.[18] Since the disappointing record of Morningstar cannot be blamed on deficiencies in the anarchist social model, neither its failure nor that of similar counter-cultural experiments impugns anarchy's value as a guide to action. The lesson of such failures is not to give up attempts to partially anarchize society, but, in making these attempts, to take as one's guide an accurate conception of the anarchist model. Since settlements and institutions rebuilt according to this model provide marked benefits without destructive havoc, it seems that between the alternatives of anarchy and incrementalism as guides to action, anarchy should be the choice.

To those who reject incrementalism for precluding the replacement of an entire social system, using anarchy to guide partial efforts to reconstruct society may seem just as unacceptable. Since the partial efforts that anarchy as a guide suggests are not appreciably bolder or more sweeping than those suggested by incrementalism, both, it may be argued, cut off the opportunities for augmenting human welfare that arise when an entire social system is replaced. It is true that the partial changes carried out under the guidance of the anarchist model have a cautious quality reminiscent of those an incrementalist would undertake. But whereas the incrementalist, being committed to the established social system, rejects measures which might jeopardize its continued existence, and confines himself to remedies for pressing, immediate evils, the anarchist, though his efforts aim to partially anarchize, not overthrow, the existing social order, finds effects of his efforts that tend to undermine that order anything but adverse. Believing that human welfare would be increased greatly if anarchy replaced the state, he welcomes the help his partial efforts give to this replacement, even though achieving it is not their point. Should the changes carried out under the guidance of his model in schools, workplaces, rural settlements and the like accumulate, as is possible, so as to completely dissolve the state, the anarchist would be delighted. Anarchy used as a guide to the partial reconstruction of society, far from evoking fear, as does incrementalism, that possibilities for wellbeing are going unfulfilled, offers the safety which is incrementalism's strong point while keeping prospects for augmenting human welfare through systemic transformation alive.[19]

Thus the worth of anarchy as a model of the best regime must be deemed outstanding, judged from a practical, as well as from a theoretical, point of view. As a complete achievement anarchy is not just possible, but offers benefits unavailable from its rivals. As a practical standard and guide, anarchy points the way to action that combines safety, immediate advantage and the promise of systemic change. Since the advice of the incrementalist to disown exigent ideals has been and no doubt always will be too severe to follow, the choice among such ideals is one that simply must be faced. Though no arguments can show that anarchy – or any ideal social model – is indisputably best, the arguments advanced in this chapter show at least that in controversy about the nature of the good society anarchy must receive a leading place.

THE SIGNIFICANCE OF ANARCHISM FOR POLITICAL THOUGHT

Recent books on anarchism all conclude with observations on its continuing vitality. Even before the Paris rebellion of May 1968, when students put anarchist theory to work in their struggles against their university and the state that lay behind it, commentators were cautioning against inferring from the rout of the anarchists in the Spanish Civil War that their theory was dead. Though none saw much hope for anarchism as an organized movement, working to replace, or even modify, the state, even the most gloomy believed that as 'an austere personal and social code' it would continue to capture the attention of receptive minds.[20] What this meant was that at least a few people could always be expected to take bearings from the anarchist tradition on how to lead their personal, aesthetic and immediate social lives. After 1968, observers began announcing with dread, triumph or amazement that the anarchist movement, transfigured by contact with the New Left, had revived.[21] These announcements of revival, because they now seem as exaggerated as the preceding reports of death, point up the hazard, which it would be foolish to defy, of forecasting anarchism's prospects. But the continued vitality of anarchism as both idea and movement prompts other less ensnaring questions, which can be answered clearly with the aid of the analysis presented in this book. What is the explanation for anarchism's longevity? And what is its significance for political thought?

The longevity of anarchism, despite its failure to win victories, or even to secure a mass following, is all the more striking when one remembers how little, as a doctrine, it has changed. The revisers of liberalism, conservatism and socialism, who often quite drastically modified the ideas they inherited in order to keep them relevant to the changing socio-economic situation of their supporters, have no anarchist counterparts. That the anarchism of the founders still intermittently revives suggests that its strength lies less than is usual with political doctrines in its appeal to interests. This suggestion is borne out by the fact that anarchism has won backing from persons whose places in society, being markedly divergent, could not all have been expected to support it, if its suitability as a medium for satisfying interests was the main source of its appeal. There have, of course, been attempts to paint anarchism as an ideology in the service of a particular class. But writers who make these attempts disagree whether it is peasants, artisans, small businessmen or rural landless workers whose interests anarchism represents. And no wonder they disagree, for anarchism has at times drawn backing from all of these groups, as well as from industrial workers.[22] The secret of anarchism's endurance, these remarks suggest, should be sought less in the support it gives to mutable class interests than in its ability to satisfy aspirations that are more universal and enduring. The black flag of anarchy, we cannot but believe, now waves above at least a corner of every human heart.

In seeking to intensify and finally to merge the individual and communal sides of life, the anarchists were following the course of much nineteenth-century political theory, exemplified, as we noted in the introduction, by Hegel and Marx. What must now be added is that these seekers on the plane of theory of a fused communal individuality were responding to concerns which, less perfectly articulated, were widespread in their culture and are even more pervasive in ours. To exhibit strong personality without losing touch with others, to unite with the whole without sinking into it, to live in a society both warmly receptive to self-expression and gratifyingly unitary – these for us are pressing aspirations. Unless one rests content with denouncing these aspirations as self-contradictory or worse, though they are central to our culture, the way that anarchists propose to satisfy them must seem filled with promise.[23] Of the various paths mapped by political theorists toward combining the fullest individual development with the greatest communal unity, that of the anarchists is distinctive in its concreteness, its immediate practicality, and in the particularized rationality and thoroughgoing liberty of its projected way of life. So long as communal individuality remains an aspiration, the path to anarchy, despite its hazards, will continue to be travelled.

NOTES

Introduction

1 Highpoints in this reassessment of anarchism as a theory are Robert Paul Wolff, *In Defense of Anarchism* (New York, 1976) and April Carter, *The Political Theory of Anarchism* (London, 1971).

2 William Proby, *Philosophy and Barbarism* (London, 1798), p. 22.

3 Benjamin Barber, *Superman and Common Men* (New York, 1972), pp. 25, 22; Isaac Kramnick, 'On Anarchism and the Real World: William Godwin and Radical England', *American Political Science Review*, 66 (March 1972), p. 116.

4 G. W. F. Hegel, *The Philosophy of Right* (Oxford, 1958), pp. 160–1, 164, 156.

5 Karl Marx, *Economic and Philosophical Manuscripts of 1844* (Moscow, 1961), pp. 108, 105. Ellen Wood has convincingly worked out Marx's views on the reciprocal relations between individuality and community: *Mind and Politics* (Berkeley, 1972), pp. 123, 141–52.

6 Patrick Riley, 'Hegel on Consent and Social-Contract Theory: Does he "Cancel and Preserve" the Will?', *Western Political Quarterly*, 26 (March 1973), especially pp. 156–61.

7 Max Stirner, *The Ego and His Own*, trans. Steven T. Byington (New York, 1963), p. 311.

8 The most recent and convincing discussions of Stirner's relationship to anarchism are to be found in R. W. K. Paterson, *The Nihilistic Egoist: Max Stirner* (Oxford, 1971), ch. VI, and John Clark, *Max Stirner's Egoism* (London, 1976), ch. VI. Both Paterson and Clark find a logical gap between Stirner's egoistic moral premise and his anarchist conclusions. Their dispute is over the issue whether his egoism or his anarchism is more characteristic of his thought and hence whether he should be called an anarchist. It should be added that though as a theorist of anarchism Stirner is a disaster, he may still deserve his recognized place in the history of anarchist ideas.

1. Liberty and public censure in anarchist thought

1 William Godwin, *Enquiry Concerning Political Justice*, 3 vols. (Toronto, 1946), II, 331; Pierre-Joseph Proudhon, *Correspondance*,

14 vols. (Paris, 1874–5), IV, 375; Michael Bakunin, *Œuvres*, 6 vols. (Paris, 1895–1913), IV, 248, 156, cf. I, 204; Peter Kropotkin, *Revolutionary Pamphlets* (New York, 1968), p. 113. All translations from French texts are my own, unless otherwise indicated. For contemporary claims that anarchists are libertarians see, for instance, Gerald Runkle, *Anarchism, Old and New* (New York, 1972), p. 165, or Derry Novak, 'The Place of Anarchism in the History of Political Thought', *The Review of Politics*, 20 (July 1958), p. 317.

2 Godwin, *Political Justice*, II, 221, 199, 274; Proudhon, *De la Justice dans la Révolution et dans l'Eglise*, 4 vols. (Paris, 1930–5), I, 315; Bakunin, *Œuvres*, III, 69n; Kropotkin, *Pamphlets*, p. 143.

3 Gerald C. MacCallum, Jr, 'Negative and Positive Freedom', *The Philosophical Review*, 76 (July 1967), pp. 312–34; cf. John Rawls, *A Theory of Justice* (Cambridge, Mass., 1972), p. 202.

4 Godwin, *Political Justice*, I, 168, II, 500; Bakunin, *Œuvres*, V, 318, cf. I, 105, 281; Proudhon, *Justice*, II, 77, cf. Proudhon, *De la capacité politique des classes ouvrières* (Paris, 1924), p. 190; Kropotkin, *Pamphlets*, p. 124.

5 For typical analysis along these lines see K. J. Scott, 'Liberty, License and Not Being Free', *Political Studies*, 4 (June 1956), pp. 176–85, or D. M. White, 'Negative Liberty', *Ethics*, 80 (April 1970), pp. 185–204.

6 Proudhon, *Justice*, III, 424.

7 Godwin, *Political Justice*, II, 496.

8 *Ibid.*, II, 434, 366–7, 505.

9 *Ibid.*, II, 340, 199.

10 Bakunin, *Œuvres*, III, 49.

11 *Ibid.*, I, 284.

12 *Ibid.*, III, 49.

13 *Ibid.*, IV, 249.

14 Proudhon, *Justice*, I, 325.

15 Bakunin, *Œuvres*, I, 284, 295; Godwin, *Political Justice*, I, 64–5, II, 499.

16 Bakunin, *Œuvres*, V, 159.

17 Godwin, *Political Justice*, II, 500; Proudhon, *Philosophie du progrès* (Paris, 1946), p. 67; Kropotkin, *La science moderne et l'anarchie* (Paris, 1913), p. 160.

18 Bakunin, *Œuvres*, III, 214, cf. I, 295, 298, V, 126, VI, 88.

19 These are the traits normally singled out as typical of a legal system. Cf. H. L. A. Hart, *The Concept of Law* (London, 1961), pp. 22–5.

20 Bakunin, *Œuvres*, I, 288; Godwin, *Political Justice*, I, 221 *inter alia*.

21 Godwin, *Political Justice*, II, 352–3.

22 *Ibid.*, II, 294; cf. 247, 399–400; Bakunin, *Œuvres*, IV, 261. The anarchists' esteem for particularity in the control of behavior must not be exaggerated. Though general rules must not be followed blindly, they have their place as presumptive guides, akin to the utilitarian's rules of thumb. It is 'incumbent on us, when called into action, to estimate the nature of the particular case, that we may ascertain

where the urgency of special circumstances is such as to supersede rules that are generally obligatory' (*Political Justice*, I, 347).

23 Kropotkin, *Pamphlets*, p. 200; cf. Godwin, *Political Justice*, II, 231, 403.

24 The penalties need not of course be identical, since some discretion in sentencing is allowed in even the least flexible legal system.

25 See ch. 4, p. 74, for a discussion of the insignificance of the differences between legal and censorial sanctions, so far as concerns their effects on satisfaction.

26 Bakunin, *Œuvres*, I, 288.

27 Godwin, *Political Justice*, II, 334, 375; Kropotkin, *Pamphlets*, pp. 157, 167; Kropotkin, *Science moderne*, pp. 160–1.

2. The goal of anarchism: communal individuality

1 George Woodcock, *Anarchism* (New York, 1962), pp. 84–5; Henri Arvon, *L'anarchisme* (Paris, 1968), p. 77; George Plekhanov, *Anarchism and Socialism* (Minneapolis, N.D.), pp. 51–2.

2 Godwin, *Enquiry Concerning Political Justice* (Toronto, 1946), II, 500; Proudhon, *De la Justice dans la Révolution et dans l'Eglise* (Paris, 1930–5), III, 253.

3 Kropotkin, *Revolutionary Pamphlets* (New York, 1968), pp. 141, 123.

4 Godwin, *Thoughts on Man* (New York, 1969), p. 310.

5 Proudhon, *Justice*, I, 414.

6 Bakunin, *Œuvres* (Paris, 1895–1913), V, 321–2.

7 Kropotkin, *Mutual Aid* (New York, 1925), p. 222.

8 Cf. Robert Paul Wolff, *The Poverty of Liberalism* (Boston, 1968), pp. 180–5.

9 Godwin, *Political Justice*, I, 258–9.

10 Proudhon, *Correspondance* (Paris, 1874–5), XI, 301 (30 December 1861); Proudhon, *Justice*, III, 411.

11 Bakunin, *Œuvres*, III, 353; Kropotkin, *Pamphlets*, pp. 139, 167.

12 Proudhon, *De la capacité politique des classes ouvrières* (Paris, 1924), p. 155.

13 Bakunin, *Œuvres*, V, 149; cf. V, 187, where Bakunin says that independence which endangers solidarity is undesirable.

14 Kropotkin, *Pamphlets*, p. 63. Evidence that anarchists subordinate freedom to individuality and community does not prove unmistakably that the latter are their coequal overriding aims. They might rank others still higher. But since they do not say they do, since freedom is so often presumed to be their chief goal, and since they consider individuality and community to have greater worth, it is reasonable to say that they give them first place.

15 The problem of resolving the conflict, so troubling to anarchists, between the claims of individuality and community is a version of the general problem in moral philosophy of how to relate the claims of the self to the claims of others. The anarchists' position on how to

reconcile individuality and community might therefore be an alternative to more familiar views such as utilitarianism or Kantianism of how the conflict between self and others should be resolved. Examined from this perspective, which is not that of this book, anarchism might have value as a theory of ethics.

16 Bakunin, *Œuvres*, V, 150, 159; cf. IV, 385.
17 Godwin, *Political Justice*, II, 486; Proudhon, *Justice*, I, 304–5, 421, III, 253, IV, 302, *Capacité*, p. 222; Kropotkin, *Pamphlets*, pp. 5, 96, 141; Kropotkin, *Selected Writings on Anarchism and Revolution*, ed. Martin Miller (Cambridge, Mass., 1970), p. 297.
18 Godwin, *Political Justice*, I, 356.
19 Bakunin, *Œuvres*, V, 150; cf. Proudhon, *Justice*, IV, 264.
20 Proudhon, *Justice*, III, 253; Kropotkin, *Selected Writings*, p. 297.
21 Kropotkin, *La science moderne et l'anarchie* (Paris, 1913), p. 332.
22 Marc Guyeau, *Esquisse d'une morale sans obligation ni sanction* (Paris, 1893), pp. 96, 98. See Kropotkin, *Pamphlets*, p. 108, for Kropotkin's judgment on Guyeau.
23 Derry Novak, 'Une lettre inédite de Pierre Kropotkine à Max Nettlau', *International Review of Social History*, 9 (1964), p. 274.
24 Godwin, *Political Justice*, II, 295; cf., II, 505.
25 *Ibid.*, I, 311; cf. Kropotkin, *Pamphlets*, p. 96.
26 Bakunin, *Œuvres*, III, 235, 253, IV, 248; Proudhon, *Justice*, III, 253; Godwin, *Political Justice*, II, 409.
27 Godwin, *Political Justice*, II, 486.
28 *Ibid.*, II, 216.
29 *Ibid.*, I, 329–30; cf. Proudhon, *Justice*, IV, 366; Bakunin, *Œuvres*, I, 181, 277, V, 321. I would still have *some* self-image since, as indicated earlier (cf. ch. 1, p. 16), spontaneous social pressure, not deliberate censure, suffices to create a self.
30 Proudhon, 'Cours d'économie politique', I–12(4) unpublished manuscript. Reference to the page number is assigned to the manuscript by Pierre Haubtmann in his unpublished thesis 'La philosophie sociale de Pierre-Joseph Proudhon' (Faculté des lettres et des sciences humaines de Paris, 1961); Bakunin, *Œuvres*, I, 290.
31 Bakunin, *Œuvres*, I, 278.
32 Proudhon, 'Cours', I–7(6). It must be admitted that this part of their argument fails to show that individuality is best supported by deliberate censure as contrasted with spontaneous social pressure.
33 Godwin, *Political Justice*, II, 273–4; Kropotkin, *Pamphlets*, p. 137.
34 Godwin, *Political Justice*, I, 340.
35 *Ibid.*, II, 497.
36 *Ibid.*, II, 500.
37 *Ibid.*, I, 137.
38 Proudhon, *Justice*, III, 175, cf. I, 316, 395, 423, IV, 264.
39 Kropotkin, *Pamphlets*, p. 109.
40 Godwin, *Political Justice*, I, 333; Kropotkin, *Pamphlets*, p. 140.
41 Godwin, *Political Justice*, I, 335.

42 Kropotkin, *Pamphlets*, pp. 53, 95.
43 Godwin, *Political Justice*, I, 179–80, II, 340–1, 374; Proudhon, *Justice*, IV, 371.

3. Varieties of anarchy

1 Godwin, *Enquiry Concerning Political Justice* (Toronto, 1946), II, 500; cf. I, 232, 236; II, 215, 497; Godwin, *The Enquirer* (New York, 1965), p. 77.
2 Godwin, *Political Justice*, I, 500; cf. Godwin, *The Enquirer*, p. 344.
3 Godwin, *Political Justice*, II, 280.
4 *Ibid.*, II, 504. For a restatement of the view that Godwin has no place 'within the philosophy of the anarchist community' see R. A. Nisbet, *The Social Philosophers* (New York, 1973), pp. 365–6.
5 Godwin, *Political Justice*, II, 504.
6 *Ibid.*, II, 505.
7 *Ibid.*, I, 295; cf. Godwin, *Thoughts on Man* (New York, 1969), p. 310 and Godwin, *The Enquirer*, pp. vii–viii, where Godwin describes the liberating effects of his own conversations.
8 Godwin, *The Enquirer*, p. 343; cf. Yvon Belaval, *Le souci de sincérité* (Paris, 1944), pp. 127–9.
9 Charles Horton Cooley, *Human Nature and the Social Order* (New York, 1902), pp. 178, 153. Cooley admits that character need not depend immediately on interaction, but he denies that it depends on reasoned thought (pp. 205–7).
10 Godwin, *Political Justice*, I, 328.
11 *Ibid.*, I, 335.
12 *Ibid.*, I, 327–8, 332, 336.
13 *Ibid.*, I, 333.
14 *Ibid.*, I, 330.
15 *Ibid.*, I, 330.
16 *Ibid.*, I, 296, 356.
17 Stuart Hampshire, 'Sincerity and Single-Mindedness', in *Freedom of Mind and Other Essays* (Princeton, 1971), p. 234; cf. Jean Starobinski, *J.-J. Rousseau, La transparence et l'obstacle* (Paris, 1971), pp. 237–8, Belaval, *Sincérité*, pp. 55, 63.
18 Godwin, *Political Justice*, I, 280, 294, 333–4, 340, Godwin, *The Enquirer*, p. 344.
19 Belaval, *Sincérité*, pp. 134–5, 177.
20 *Ibid.*, p. 144, Starobinski, *J.-J. Rousseau*, p. 188, George Santayana, 'The Comic Mask', in *Soliloquies on England and Later Soliloquies* (New York, 1922), p. 135.
21 Godwin, *The Enquirer*, pp. 341, 349; cf. Godwin, *Thoughts on Man*, pp. 301–4; Godwin, *Political Justice*, I, 348–9.
22 Nietzsche, *Beyond Good and Evil* (Chicago, 1955), section 40.
23 Santayana, *Soliloquies*, p. 133.
24 Belaval, *Sincérité*, p. 165; Lionel Trilling, *Sincerity and Authenticity* (Cambridge, Mass., 1972), p. 119; Paul A. Freund, 'Privacy: One

Concept or Many', in J. Roland Pennock and John W. Chapman (eds.), *Privacy* (New York, 1971), p. 195; John R. Silber, 'Masks and Fig Leaves', *ibid.*, p. 233.

25 Quoted in Belaval, *Sincérité*, p. 120.

26 Kurt H. Wolff (ed.), *The Sociology of Georg Simmel* (New York, 1964), p. 329.

27 Freund, 'Privacy', p. 195; Alan E. Westin, *Privacy and Freedom* (New York, 1967), p. 37.

28 Godwin, *Political Justice*, I, 332, II, 275.

29 *Ibid.*, II, 505–6: To 'the most perfect man...society is not a necessary of life but a luxury...He will resort with scarcely inferior eagerness to solitude; and will find in it the highest complacence and the purest delight.' For evidence that Godwin values discretion as contrasted with reserve see Godwin, *The Enquirer*, p. 127.

30 Proudhon, *De la Justice dans la Révolution et dans l'Eglise* (Paris, 1930–5), III, 253; Bakunin, *Œuvres* (Paris, 1895–1913), I, 101, 105.

31 Bakunin, *Œuvres*, I, 221.

32 Proudhon, *Justice*, III, 88; cf. Bakunin, *Œuvres*, I, 109–10, V, 204.

33 Proudhon, *Justice*, III, 69–70; Bakunin, *Œuvres*, I, 109.

34 Proudhon, *Justice*, III, 256; cf. I, 436.

35 For a detailed analysis of Proudhon's anarchist society see Alan Ritter, *The Political Thought of Pierre-Joseph Proudhon* (Princeton, 1969), pp. 126–34; a good text describing Bakunin's social vision is in *Œuvres*, II, 297.

36 Proudhon, *Justice*, III, 87–8; Bakunin, 'Revolutionary Catechism', in Sam Dolgoff (ed.), *Bakunin on Anarchy* (New York, 1971), pp. 89–93.

37 Proudhon, *Justice*, III, 86; for Bakunin's description of 'integral education', which is very close to Proudhon's polytechnical apprenticeship, see *Œuvres*, V, 136, 145, 156–7.

38 Proudhon, *Justice*, III, 87–8.

39 *Ibid.*, III, 92–3. Though this description of an anarchist economy is based solely on what Proudhon writes, Bakunin agrees with it. He is less specific in his economic plans, but what he says, such as that no one may devote himself exclusively to manual or mental work (*Œuvres*, V, 126–8, I, 360), shows that he encourages communal individuality with the same practice of occupational mobility used by Proudhon.

40 Bakunin, 'Revolutionary Catechism', in Dolgoff, *Bakunin on Anarchy*, p. 95.

41 *Ibid.*, p. 94, cf. *Œuvres*, I, 317.

42 Proudhon, *Justice*, IV, 271, 283.

43 *Ibid.*, IV, 322.

44 *Ibid.*, IV, 274.

45 That Proudhon finds much communal individuality in the family is shown by where he puts the figure of a mirror. It is a mother or wife who, 'transparent and luminous, serves man as the mirror...in which to contemplate his character' (*Justice*, IV, 266, 268). Bakunin follows

Godwin in finding that members of society, not the family, best reflect the self (*Œuvres*, V, 321).

46 Proudhon, *Justice*, I, 301, 418; Bakunin, *Œuvres*, I, 117, V, 309; cf. R. S. Downie and Elizabeth Telfer, *Respect for Persons* (New York, 1970), especially ch. 1, and Bernard Williams, 'The Idea of Equality', reprinted in Hugo A. Bedau (ed.), *Justice and Equality* (New York, 1971), especially pp. 123–4.
47 Proudhon, *Justice*, I, 419.
48 Proudhon, *Idée générale de la révolution au dix-neuvième siècle* (Paris, 1923), p. 189.
49 Proudhon, *Justice*, I, 417; cf. Downie and Telfer, *Respect*, pp. 21, 25.
50 Kropotkin, *Revolutionary Pamphlets* (New York, 1968), p. 107; cf. p. 105 for Kropotkin's acknowledgment of the value of respect.
51 *Ibid.*, p. 107; cf. Derry Novak, 'Une lettre inédite de Pierre Kropotkine à Max Nettlau', *International Review of Social History*, 9 (1964), p. 272.
52 Kropotkin, *Mutual Aid* (New York, 1925), p. 205.
53 *Ibid.*, p. 211.
54 Kropotkin, *Pamphlets*, pp. 109, 141, 123.
55 *Ibid.*, p .109.
56 *Ibid.*, p. 109.
57 *Ibid.*, pp. 139, 140, 108. It is important to note that though Kropotkin envisages community as occurring in both domestic and social life, he does not want it to be the same in both. He warns not to 'take the family as a model' for relations in larger, less intimate groups. 'Communisme et anarchie', in *La science moderne et l'anarchie* (Paris, 1913), p. 144, cf. p. 153.
58 Kropotkin, *Pamphlets*, p. 95.
59 *Ibid.*, pp. 123–4.

4. The anarchists as critics of established institutions

1 See, for instance, Gerald Runkle, *Anarchism: Old and New* (New York, 1972), p. 168; James Joll, *The Anarchists* (London, 1964), p. 278; George Woodcock, *Anarchism* (New York, 1962), p. 469.
2 Robert Paul Wolff, *In Defense of Anarchism* (New York, 1976), pp. 22–7. The conflation of anarchism and radical democracy is common; for an elaborate example see Richard T. DeGeorge, 'Anarchism and Authority', in J. Roland Pennock and John Chapman (eds.), *Anarchism: Nomos XIX* (New York, 1978), pp. 91–110. In his 'Reply to Reiman' Wolff takes back his claim that anarchism and unanimous direct democracy are compatible (*In Defense of Anarchism*, p. 88).
3 Godwin, *Enquiry Concerning Political Justice* (Toronto, 1946), I, 297.
4 *Ibid.*, II, 204.
5 Proudhon, *Du principe fédératif* (Paris, 1959), p. 344; Godwin, *Political Justice*, I, 297.
6 Godwin, *Political Justice*, II, 145.
7 Bakunin, *Œuvres* (Paris, 1895–1913), IV, 476, cf. I, 156.

8 See, for instance, W. D. Handcock, 'The Function and Nature of Authority in Society', *Philosophy*, 28 (April 1953), p. 101.

9 Proudhon, for instance, takes a patriarchal stand reminiscent of Filmer on the issue of domestic authority, while Godwin and Bakunin follow Plato in defending the authority of experts over private action and belief. Godwin, *Political Justice*, I, 236; Proudhon, *De la Justice dans la Révolution et dans l'Eglise*, IV, 322; Bakunin, *Œuvres*, III, 55.

10 For evidence that anarchists accept this understanding of authority see Godwin, *Political Justice*, I, 121; Proudhon, *Justice*, II, 312; Kropotkin, *Revolutionary Pamphlets* (New York, 1968), p. 217.

11 Godwin, *Political Justice*, I, 227, 234; Bakunin, *Œuvres*, III, 55.

12 Godwin, *Political Justice*, I, 235; cf. I, 215 and Kropotkin, *Pamphlets*, pp. 58–9.

13 Godwin, *Political Justice*, I, 234–5.

14 *Ibid.*, I, 121, 212; Proudhon, *Justice*, II, 226, 310; Bakunin, *Œuvres*, III, 49–54; Kropotkin, *Pamphlets*, 147, 217.

15 Godwin, *Political Justice*, I, 181; cf. Bakunin, *Œuvres*, V, 313; Proudhon, *Justice*, I, 326, IV, 350; Kropotkin, *Pamphlets*, pp. 167, 285.

16 Proudhon, *Justice*, II, 218; Bakunin, *Œuvres*, III, 69n.

17 Godwin, *Political Justice*, II, 211, 340.

18 Proudhon, *Justice*, II, 218, 262; Bakunin, *Œuvres*, III, 60; Godwin, *Political Justice*, II, 496. A situation where everybody has public authority over everybody else is difficult to grasp. What happens, for instance, if two members of an anarchy issue contradictory directives? Which one has the right to be obeyed? The anarchists evade answering this question. Perhaps all that can be said is that since directives in an anarchy are only issued to correct serious misconduct, which is infrequent, and obvious to all, conflicts among directives are unlikely.

19 Godwin, *Political Justice*, II, 294, 399–400.

20 *Ibid.*, II, 363, Proudhon, *Justice*, IV, 373.

21 Godwin, *Political Justice*, II, 334.

22 *Ibid.*, II, 340–1.

23 *Ibid.*, II, 345.

24 *Ibid.*, II, 379. For more detail on this point see Alan Ritter, 'Godwin, Proudhon and the Anarchist Justification of Punishment', *Political Theory*, 3 (February 1975), p. 83.

25 Godwin, *Political Justice*, II, 322; cf. Proudhon, *Idée générale de la révolution au dix-neuvième siècle* (Paris, 1923), pp. 311–12, *Justice*, IV, 371.

26 Godwin, *Political Justice*, II, 349 on vengeance, II, 322, 334, 365–6 on self-defense; Proudhon, *Idée générale*, p. 311 on vengeance.

27 Godwin, *Political Justice*, II, 199.

28 Proudhon, *Justice*, IV, 377.

29 *Ibid.*

30 Godwin, *Political Justice*, II, 361, cf. II, 340.

31 Writers who call anarchists radical egalitarians include Isaiah Berlin, 'Equality as an Ideal', in Frederick A. Olafson (ed.), *Justice and*

Social Policy (Englewood Cliffs, N.J., 1961), pp. 141–2, and Felix Oppenheim, 'Egalitarianism as a Descriptive Concept', *American Philosophical Quarterly*, 7 (April 1970), p. 144.

32 Godwin, *Political Justice*, II, 453.
33 *Ibid.*, II, 430, 454, 461.
34 *Ibid.*, II, 460, 465.
35 *Ibid.*, I, 23.
36 *Ibid.*, II, 463.
37 *Ibid.*, II, 429.
38 *Ibid.*, I, 147.
39 *Ibid.*, II, 422, 450.
40 *Ibid.*, II, 93.
41 For a developed argument that the criterion of need is egalitarian see Gregory Vlastos, 'Justice and Equality', in Richard B. Brant (ed.), *Social Justice* (Englewood Cliffs, N.J., 1962), pp. 42–3.
42 Godwin, *Political Justice*, II, 423–4; cf. I, 448.
43 *Ibid.*, II, 433, 428.
44 Kropotkin, *The Conquest of Bread* (New York, 1969), pp. 230–1; cf. p. 8.
45 *Ibid.*, pp. 63–4.
46 *Ibid.*, p. 233.
47 Kropotkin, 'Communisme et anarchie', in *Science moderne*, p. 166; Kropotkin, *The Conquest of Bread*, p. 227. For a more thorough analysis of Kropotkin on justice see David Miller, *Social Justice* (Oxford, 1976), pp. 209–52.
48 'Equality does not imply the leveling of individual differences, nor that individuals should be made physically, morally or mentally identical. Diversity in capacities and powers, . . .far from being a social evil, constitutes on the contrary, the abundance of humanity.' Bakunin, 'Revolutionary Catechism', in Dolgoff (ed.), *Bakunin on Anarchy*, pp. 87–8.
49 Proudhon, *Système de contradictions économiques*, 2 vols. (Paris, 1923), I, 191.
50 Bakunin, *Œuvres*, IV, 477.
51 Kropotkin, *The Conquest of Bread*, pp. 127, 136–9.
52 *Ibid.*, p. 153. Kropotkin would not confine consumption of *all* luxuries to their producers; some, such as books, though cooperatively produced by everyone, from author to pressman, who helped create them, would be available to all. Kropotkin does not say how to distinguish between luxuries which should be open to general consumption and luxuries which should be consumed by their producers only.
53 Kropotkin, *Fields, Factories and Workshops* (New York, 1909), pp. 3–4; cf. pp. v–vi.
54 *Ibid.*, pp. 161, 178, 180.
55 *Ibid.* (enlarged edn, New York, 1968), pp. 358–60.
56 Industrial technology should only be controlled, according to Marxists, when it becomes a fetter, *after* capitalism has ceased to be progressive. To control it before then, as anarchists suggest, would only delay

the advent of the socialist revolution by arresting the development of productive forces.

5. Anarchist strategy: the dilemma of means and ends

1 Many writers have equated anarchist strategy with terrorism, e.g. George Plekhanov, *Anarchism and Socialism*; a balanced discussion of this matter is Derry Novak, 'Anarchism and Individual Terrorism', *Canadian Journal of Political Science*, 20 (May 1954), pp. 176–84. For a 'gallery of outlandish stereotypes' see Leonard Krimmerman and Lewis Perry (eds.), *Patterns of Anarchy* (New York, 1966), pp. xvi–xvii. In a single paragraph David Apter manages to ascribe all these strategies and more to the anarchists: 'The Old Anarchism and the New – Some Comments', *Government and Opposition*, 5 (Autumn 1970), p. 397. E. J. Hobsbawm calls anarchists revolutionary voluntarists both in *Primitive Rebels* (New York, 1959), p. 83, and in *Revolutionaries* (New York, 1973), p. 86.

2 Good examples of the interpretation of anarchist strategy as non-political may be found in George Woodcock, *Anarchism* (New York, 1962), p. 31, and Isaac Kramnick, 'On Anarchism and the Real World: William Godwin and Radical England', *American Political Science Review*, 66 (March 1972), p. 128.

3 Bakunin, *Œuvres* (Paris, 1895–1913), V, 208.

4 Irving L. Horowitz (ed.), *The Anarchists* (New York, 1964), p. 29.

5 Godwin, *Enquiry Concerning Political Justice* (Toronto, 1946), I, 279.

6 *Ibid.*, I, 272.

7 *Ibid.*, I, 289.

8 *Ibid.*, I, 221.

9 *Ibid.*, I, 78, 83.

10 *Ibid.*, I, 69.

11 *Ibid.*, I, 49.

12 *Ibid.*, II, 225.

13 *Ibid.*, II, 243–4.

14 *Ibid.*, I, 273.

15 *Ibid.*, I, 256.

16 *Ibid.*, II, 243.

17 *Ibid.*, II, 372.

18 *Ibid.*, II, 491–2.

19 *Ibid.*, I, 278, cf. II, 549.

20 *Ibid.*, I, 104.

21 *Ibid.*, I, 296.

22 *Ibid.*, II, 209–12; for more detail on these steps toward Godwinian anarchy see John P. Clark, *The Philosophical Anarchism of William Godwin* (Princeton, 1977), pp. 191–4.

23 Kramnick, 'Anarchism and the Real World', pp. 126, 114.

24 'The true reason why the mass of mankind has so often been the dupe of knaves, has been the mysterious and complicated nature of the social system. Once annihilate the quackery of government, and the

most homebred understanding might be strong enough to detect the artifices of the state juggler that would mislead him.' Godwin, *Political Justice*, II, 208, cf. II, 136–7.

25 *Ibid.*, II, 477.
26 *Ibid.*, I, 298.
27 *Ibid.*, I, 274.
28 Proudhon, *Système de contradictions économiques* (Paris, 1923), II, 403.
29 Proudhon, *Idée générale de la révolution au dix-neuvième siècle* (Paris, 1923), p. 374.
30 Proudhon, *Les carnets*, 4 vols. (Paris, 1960–74), III, 45. For the more detailed analysis of Proudhon's strategy on which this account is based see Ritter, *The Political Thought of Proudhon*, ch. VI.
31 Proudhon, *Qu'est-ce que la propriété?* (Paris, 1926), p. 345.
32 Proudhon, *Mélanges*, 3 vols. (Paris, 1868–70), III, 123; Proudhon, *La révolution sociale démontrée par le coup d'état du deux décembre* (Paris, 1936), p. 206.
33 Proudhon, *Carnets*, III, 248; Proudhon, *Mélanges*, II, 1.
34 Proudhon, *La révolution sociale*, p. 177.
35 Proudhon, *De la Justice dans la Révolution et dans l'Eglise* (Paris, 1930–5), IV, 468.
36 *Ibid.*, IV, 489.
37 Proudhon, *Correspondance* (Paris, 1874–5), IX, 71.
38 Proudhon, *De la capacité politique des classes ouvrières* (Paris, 1924), p. 236.
39 *Ibid.*, p. 74.
40 *Ibid.*, p. 240; cf. p. 101.
41 'Has there ever been a single example, at any time in any place, of a privileged, dominant class making concessions freely, spontaneously, without being forced to by coercion and fear?' Bakunin, *Œuvres*, VI, 359–60.
42 'Rapport de la commission sur la question de l'héritage', Bakunin, *Œuvres*, V, 199–210.
43 Marx, Engels and Lenin, *Anarchism and Anarcho-Syndicalism* (New York, 1972), pp. 45–6.
44 Bakunin, *Œuvres*, I, 173, 296, II, 46, 335.
45 *Ibid.*, III, 64 note.
46 *Ibid.*, II, 423.
47 *Ibid.*, II, 101; Arthur Lehning (ed.), *Michael Bakunin, Selected Writings* (New York, 1973), p. 168. Cf. Daniel Guerin (ed.), *Ni Dieu ni maître* (Lausanne, N.D.), p. 202.
48 Lehning, *Selected Writings*, p. 169.
49 Bakunin, *Œuvres*, VI, 70–2.
50 *Ibid.*, IV, 260.
51 Godwin, *Political Justice*, I, 274.
52 Kropotkin, *Fields, Factories and Workshops* (New York, 1913), pp. 394–402.
53 Kropotkin, *Paroles d'un révolté* (Paris, 1885), pp. 308–9, 310; cf.

Kropotkin, *Revolutionary Pamphlets* (New York, 1968), p. 156.
54 Kropotkin, *Pamphlets*, p. 185. Cf. Martin A. Miller, *Kropotkin* (Chicago, 1976), p. 191. Kropotkin rejected 'a vanguard elite which would operate either before or after the revolution'.
55 For a good account of Kropotkin's early anarchism, see Miller, *Kropotkin*, pp. 146, 174–5.
56 Kropotkin, *Paroles*, p. 122.
57 Kropotkin, *Pamphlets*, pp. 51, 68.
58 *Ibid.*, p. 35.
59 *Ibid.*, pp. 35–43. Quotation from this essay fails to capture its force. It should be read in its entirety.
60 *Ibid.*, p. 188.
61 Kropotkin, *The Conquest of Bread* (New York, 1969), p. 57.
62 For a detailed scenario see Kropotkin, *The Conquest of Bread*, chs. 4–7.
63 Proudhon's epigraph for his *Système de contradictions économiques* was 'Destruam et Aedificabo'. Bakunin insisted throughout his life that 'the passion for destruction is a creative passion, too'. Lehning, *Selected Writings*, p. 58.
64 Kropotkin, *The Conquest of Bread*, pp. 109–10.
65 *Ibid.*, p. 80.
66 Daniel Guerin, *Anarchism* (New York, 1970), p. 38.
67 For a fine elaboration of these points see George Kateb, *Utopia and its Enemies* (Glencoe, Ill., 1963), pp. 44–6.

6. The place of anarchism in the spectrum of political ideas

1 Oscar Jaszi, 'Anarchism', in *The Encyclopedia of the Social Sciences*, 2 (New York, 1937), p. 52; Daniel Guerin, *Anarchism* (New York, 1970), p. 12; cf. Noam Chomsky's introduction, p. xv.
2 William H. Hocking, *Man and the State* (New Haven, 1926), pp. 97, 91.
3 Immanuel Kant, *The Metaphysical Elements of Justice*, ed. John Ladd (Indianapolis, 1965), pp. 43–4.
4 Benjamin Constant, *Œuvres* (Paris, 1957), p. 1232.
5 Mill's case is difficult. For discussion of the normative status of freedom in his theory see Robert Paul Wolff, *The Poverty of Liberalism* (Boston, 1968), pp. 19–20; Albert W. Levi, 'The Value of Freedom: Mill's "Liberty" (1859–1959)', reprinted in Peter Radcliff (ed.), *Limits of Liberty* (Belmont, Calif., 1966), pp. 6–18; H. J. McCloskey, 'Mill's Liberalism', reprinted in Isaac Kramnick (ed.), *Essays in the History of Political Thought* (New York, 1969), p. 373.
6 Kant, *Metaphysical Elements of Justice*, p. 19.
7 Godwin: 'The man who is acquainted with all the circumstances under which a living or intelligent being is placed upon any given occasion is qualified to predict the conduct he will hold with as much certainty as he can predict any of the phenomena of inanimate nature.' *Enquiry Concerning Political Justice* (Toronto, 1946), I, 363. Bakunin: Man 'is irrevocably chained to the natural and social world

of which he is a product and in which, like everything that exists, after having been an effect, and continuing to be one, he becomes in turn a relative cause of relatively new products'. *Œuvres* (Paris, 1895–1913), III, 253. Kropotkin: 'Anarchism is a world-concept based upon a mechanical explanation of all phenomena, embracing the whole of nature – that is, including in it the life of human societies.' *Revolutionary Pamphlets* (New York, 1968), p. 150.

8   Jeremy Bentham, *Introduction to the Principles of Morals and Legislation* (New York, 1948), p. 170.

9   For the argument that Godwin is a utilitarian see D. H. Monro, *Godwin's Moral Philosophy* (London, 1953), pp. 14–20, and John P. Clark, *The Philosophical Anarchism of William Godwin* (Princeton, N.J., 1977), pp. 93–126. J. B. Priestley's case against calling Godwin a utilitarian is unconvincing. See his edition of *Political Justice* (Toronto, 1946), III, 15–16.

10   Kropotkin, *Pamphlets*, p. 153.

11   Kropotkin, *Ethics* (New York, 1924), pp. 239, 241.

12   Proudhon, *De la Justice dans la Révolution et dans l'Eglise* (Paris, 1930–5), III, 544; cf. I, 310.

13   *Ibid.*, III, 444.

14   Godwin, *Political Justice*, II, 500.

15   Kropotkin, *Pamphlets*, p. 123.

16   See Wolff, *The Poverty of Liberalism*, pp. 183–5, and, for a more nuanced view, Gerald F. Gaus and John W. Chapman, 'Anarchism and Political Philosophy: An Introduction', in J. Roland Pennock and John W. Chapman (eds.), *Anarchism* (New York, 1978), p. xxxi. Wolff overstates a good case. There are signs of devotion to community among some liberals, but they are faint and leave little mark on the practices of liberal society. Certainly, liberals do not seek communal individuality above all else. For evidence of Mill's concern for community see *On Liberty* (Indianapolis, 1956), p. 76.

17   Immanuel Kant, *The Philosophy of Kant*, ed. Carl J. Friedrich (New York, 1949), p. 120. For some astute remarks on Locke's psychology, see Gordon J. Schochet, 'The Family and the Origins of the State in Locke's Political Philosophy', in John Yolton (ed.), *John Locke: Problems and Perspectives* (Cambridge, England, 1968), pp. 95–6.

18   Proudhon, *Justice*, I, 416; cf. *La guerre et la paix* (Paris, 1927), pp. 118–21.

19   Bakunin, *Œuvres*, I, 137.

20   As John Clark aptly demonstrates. See 'What is Anarchism?', in Pennock and Chapman (eds.), *Anarchism*, pp. 15–17.

21   Godwin, *Thoughts on Man* (New York, 1969), pp. 97, 12, 112.

22   Godwin, *Political Justice*, I, 94; cf. *Political Justice*, I, 184; II, 533; and Monro, *Godwin's Moral Philosophy*, pp. 167, 172–82. Charles Frankel in *The Case For Modern Man* (Boston, 1959), pp. 102–6, shows the sobriety of Condorcet's doctrine of perfectibility. Much of what is there said of Condorcet also applies to Godwin.

23   Kropotkin, *Pamphlets*, p. 218; cf. p. 106 where Kropotkin says that

even in an anarchy it may be a man's 'bent of character' to deceive his friends.

24 Bertrand de Jouvenel discusses them in *Sovereignty* (Chicago, 1957), pp. 130–5.

25 Thomas Paine, *The Selected Works of Tom Paine and Citizen Tom Paine*, ed. Howard Fast (New York, 1943), p. 90.

26 It is true that he relied more heavily on the moral sanction in his pages on indirect legislation, but he never published them and it is unclear how seriously he took them. On this question see Mary P. Mack, *Jeremy Bentham: An Odyssey of Ideas* (New York, 1963), pp. 170–3.

27 Benjamin Constant, *Cours de politique constitutionelle*, ed. Edouard Laboulaye (Paris, 1861), II, 554.

28 Cf. James M. Buchanan, 'A Contractarian Perspective on Anarchy', in Pennock and Chapman (eds.), *Anarchism*, p. 29. 'I have often described myself as a philosophical anarchist. In my conceptualized ideal society individuals with well defined and mutually respected rights coexist and cooperate as they desire without formal political structure. My practical ideal, however, moves one stage down from this and is based on the presumption that individuals could not attain the behavioral standards required for such anarchy to function acceptably. In general recognition of this frailty in human nature, persons would agree to enact laws, and to provide means of enforcement, so as to achieve the closest approximation that is possible to the ideally free society.'

This is the place to acknowledge the existence in America of anarchists, beginning with Josiah Warren, culminating with Benjamin Tucker, and exemplified at present by figures such as David Friedman or Murray Rothbard, who, unlike the anarchists being studied in this book, must be classified as liberals. These anarchists – often denominated individualists – differ from the founders in seeing a conflict between individuality and community and in resolving the conflict by giving individuality precedence. The friendly criticism of anarchists advanced by writers like Buchanan, though misguided if seen as aimed at the founders, is on target as applied to these individualists. It is indeed naive to claim that individuality can flourish without the bonds of either community or the state.

29 On Marx as a seeker of communal individuality see above, Introduction.

30 Which doesn't apply to socialism before 1848. Cf. G. D. H. Cole, *A History of Socialist Thought*, vol. I (London, 1959), pp. 131, 313.

31 Avineri illuminatingly equates Marx's use of 'political' here with 'partial'. Shlomo Avineri, *The Social and Political Thought of Karl Marx* (Cambridge, England, 1968), p. 212.

32 Marx, Engels and Lenin, *Anarchism and Anarcho-Syndicalism* (New York, 1972), pp. 168, 150.

33 *Ibid.*, p. 150.

34 Other interpreters of Marxism who agree that a state remains in the highest stage of socialism include Richard Adamiak, 'The Withering

Away of the State: A Reconsideration', *Journal of Politics*, 32 (February 1970), pp. 3–18; Thilo Ramm, 'Die Künftige Gesellschaftsordnung nach der Theorie von Marx und Engels', in Iring Fetscher (ed.), *Marxismusstudien*, vol. II (Tübingen, 1957), pp. 77–119, see especially p. 102; John Plamenatz, *Man and Society*, 2 vols. (London, 1963), II, 373: 'Marx and Engels...made a distinction between *government* and *administration*, predicting the disappearance in the classless society of only the first. Though they did not...make it clear just what this distinction amounts to, they seem to have included in administration some of the activities usually called governmental.'

35 *Misère de la philosophie*, ed. Henri Mougin (Paris, 1961), p. 153.

36 Godwin, *Political Justice*, II, 463, 443, 466.

37 Proudhon, *Justice*, III, 174; Bakunin, *Œuvres*, II, 108, IV, 407, V, 312; Kropotkin, *Pamphlets*, p. 166.

38 Consider this criticism by Bakunin of Marx. Marx 'says that "hardship produces political slavery – the State", but does not allow for the converse: "Political slavery – the State – reproduces and maintains hardship as a condition of its existence"'. Arthur Lehning (ed.), *Michael Bakunin: Selected Writings* (New York, 1973), p. 256. Though the state, for Marx, has more causal independence than Bakunin allows, it is still far more dependent on the economy than it is for Bakunin, or any anarchist.

39 Godwin, *Political Justice*, II, 2; Bakunin, *Œuvres*, II, 327; Proudhon, *Confessions d'un révolutionnaire* (Paris, 1929), p. 215.

40 Avineri, *Social and Political Thought of Marx*, pp. 202–20.

41 For instance, 'Universal suffrage, so long as it is exercised in a society where the people, the working masses, are economically dominated by a minority,...can never produce anything but illusory elections, which are anti-democratic and absolutely opposed to the needs, instincts and real will of the population.' (Bakunin, *Œuvres*, II, 311) Bakunin, being for once more careful than the other anarchists, excepts the people of Britain and the United States from his strictures. In these countries, 'the freedom of the masses and their capacity for political action have reached the highest level of development known to history'. (IV, 449) Yet their enlightenment is for Bakunin no sign that the support of the British or American masses should be sought in an election. 'Their political consciousness, having reached its zenith, and having produced all of its fruits, is obviously tending to become transformed into the anti-political consciousness of the anarchists.' (IV, 451)

42 The conflict between anarchists and socialists on this point is nowhere better exemplified than in one of Marx's marginal notes on Bakunin's *Statism and Anarchy*. Bakunin had complained that the officials of the state envisioned by the Marxists would not build socialism, for they would be 'ex-workers, who, once they become rulers or representatives of the people, cease to be workers'. To this Marx replied, 'No more than a manufacturer today ceases to be a capitalist when he becomes a member of the municipal council'.

Henry Mayer (ed.), 'Karl Marx: Marginal Notes on Bakunin's "Statism and Anarchy"', *Etudes de Marxologie*, x (October 1959), pp. 112–13. A slightly different version is included in Marx, Engels, Lenin, *Anarchism and Anarcho-Syndicalism*, pp. 147–52.

43 Noam Chomsky, 'Introduction' to Guerin, *Anarchism*, p. xii.
44 *Ibid.*, p. xvii. All aspects of this contrast are based on Chomsky's remarks.
45 *Ibid.*, p. xv.

7. Evaluating anarchism

1 Kropotkin, 'The State: Its Historical Role', in Miller (ed.), *Selected Writings on Anarchism and Revolution* (Cambridge, Mass., 1970), *Mutual Aid* (New York, 1925), chs. 3–8, *Revolutionary Pamphlets* (New York, 1968), pp. 65–6. For recent work by an anthropologist who reaches conclusions similar to Kropotkin's about the anarchistic quality of some primitive societies see Pierre Clastres, *Society Against the State* (New York, 1977); and for a recent report on the Royal National Life-Boat Institution see *The New York Times* (23 April 1978). The coxswain of the Dover lifeboat is quoted as saying, 'This job is much too important to let the Government get its hands on it.'

2 Edward Hyndman, *The Historical Basis of Socialism in England* (London, 1883), p. 425. Donald McIntosh, 'The Dimensions of Anarchy', in Pennock and Chapman (eds.), *Anarchism* (New York, 1978), p. 263.

3 Roel Van Duyn, *Message of a Wise Kabouter* (London, 1969), pp. 48–9; Laurence Veysey, *The Communal Experience* (New York, 1973), pp. 427–9. Lyman Tower Sargent, 'Social Decision Making in Anarchism and Minimalism' (unpublished paper presented at the Fifth Plenary Meeting of AMINTAPHIL, November 1976), pp. 17–18.

4 J.-J. Rousseau, *Emile*, trans. Barbara Foxley (London, 1911), p. 7.

5 Michael Walzer, *Obligations: Essays on Disobedience, War and Citizenship* (Cambridge, Mass., 1970), pp. 238, 231.

6 It must not be forgotten that the anarchists, in laying out these requirements for freedom, are concerned with action in the public sphere. They acknowledge that in acting privately, as when I build my own house, it is not irrational to follow rules or experts without verifying the merit of the particular actions they prescribe. Nor must it be forgotten that in the rational deliberation of the anarchists general rules must be consulted as presumptive guides.

7 In laying out the conditions which serve as a background to the exercise of freedom, the anarchists can be viewed as doing for liberty what is more often done for justice. Just as the theory of justice identifies the background conditions which best assure that entirely procedural adjudication will yield a just verdict, so anarchist theory identifies the background conditions which make it most likely that an entirely procedural liberty will yield good conduct.

8 The *locus classicus* for the objection is Karl Popper, *The Open Society and Its Enemies* (New York, 1962), vol. 1, ch. 9; see also his

essay, 'Utopia and Violence', in *Conjectures and Refutations* (New York, 1963), pp. 355–64.

9 Incrementalism as a decision procedure is carefully laid out by Robert Dahl and Charles Lindblom in *Politics, Economics and Welfare* (New York, 1953), pp. 82–6.

10 Godwin, *Enquiry Concerning Political Justice* (Toronto, 1946), II, 402. The last part of Kropotkin's 'Law and Authority', in *Pamphlets*, pp. 206–8, fills out this analysis.

11 Lester Mazor, 'Disrespect for Law', in Pennock and Chapman (eds.), *Anarchism*, pp. 143–59. See also the suggestive essay by Stanley Diamond, 'The Rule of Law Versus the Order of Custom', in Robert Paul Wolff (ed.), *The Rule of Law* (New York, 1971), pp. 115–44. It is important not to confuse these empirical studies of law, which criticize it from an anarchist perspective, with empirical criticism from a socialist viewpoint, a good example of which is Richard Quinney, *Critique of Legal Order* (Boston, 1973). Quinney makes no attempt to blame the suffering he documents as caused by the American legal system on law as such; the culprit for him is the capitalist economy. He says only that 'there is no need for a legal order, *as known under capitalism*, in the social relations of a socialist society', p. 191 (my emphasis).

12 Quoted in David Stafford, 'Anarchists in Britain Today', *Government and Opposition*, 5 (Autumn 1970), p. 488.

13 Bayard Boyeson, 'The Modern School', in Perry and Krimmerman, *Patterns of Anarchy* (New York, 1966), pp. 417–20. For a description of the school in a less anarchist phase, from 1920 to 1925, after it had been transferred to Stelton, New Jersey, see Veysey, *The Communal Experience*, pp. 141–8. For contemporary developments in anarchist education, including details about specific schools, see George Dennison, *The Lives of Children* (New York, 1969), Allen Graubard, *Free the Children* (New York, 1972), and Joel Spring, *A Primer of Libertarian Education* (New York, 1975).

14 Colin Ward, *Anarchy in Action* (New York, 1973), pp. 95–109. For analysis of the value and effects of self-management see Gerry Hunnius, G. David Garson and John Case (eds.), *Workers' Control* (New York, 1973), and Carole Pateman, *Participation and Democratic Theory* (Cambridge, England, 1970), ch. IV, 'Participation and "Democracy" in Industry'.

15 Charles Gide, *Communist and Cooperative Colonies* (London, 1930), pp. 157–63. Another anarchist commune founded in France during this period, and just touched upon in Gide's survey, was more thoroughly described in a contemporary newspaper account. The Aiglemont Colony, established in 1903 by Fortuné Henry, an anarchist who had spent thirteen years in prison for his earlier, less circumspect activities, followed a similar trajectory to the Colony of Vaux. According to Henry, at Aiglemont 'the only signal everyone obeys is the dinner gong'. No one commands. 'Each evening, we decide what work to do the next day; but the next day each of us does his work

just as he pleases.' The newspaper correspondent reported from Aiglemont that there were indeed no fixed rules or routines governing work, yet the settlers were producing more than enough to live on. The Aiglemont Colony fell apart, like the one at Vaux, when its founder was called a dictator and invited to leave. *Le Temps*, 11 and 13 June 1905.

16 Laurence Veysey, on whose somewhat querulous account of Stelton these remarks are based, though he concludes that the Colony's record was 'mixed and inconclusive', nevertheless is moved to add that 'to have fought the outside world for so long to a kind of draw is itself impressive'. *The Communal Experience*, p. 177.

17 Veysey, *The Communal Experience*, pp. 185–8; Richard Fairfield, *Communes U.S.A.* (Baltimore, 1972), pp. 39–52.

18 Keith Melville, *Communes in the Counter Culture* (New York, 1972), pp. 126–9; Fairfield, *Communes*, pp. 241–67.

19 Using anarchy as a guide to partial reconstruction certainly does not assure beneficial transformation, or even make it probable. The withdrawal of anarchists into separate institutions might consolidate, rather than undermine, the established social order.

20 Joll, *The Anarchists* (London, 1964), p. 279, Woodcock, *Anarchism* (New York, 1962), p. 475.

21 Karl Wittfogel responded with dread in 'Marxism, Anarchism, and the New Left' (unpublished paper presented at the annual meeting of the American Political Science Association, September 1969). For a triumphant response see Guerin, *Anarchism* (New York, 1970), 'Postscript: May, 1968', pp. 155–9, and for responses which express varied degrees of amazement see James Joll, 'Anarchism – A Living Tradition', *Government and Opposition*, 5 (Autumn 1970), pp. 541–54, and Gerald Runkel, *Anarchism: Old and New* (New York, 1972), pp. 175–220.

22 Pre-eminently, the members of the Spanish CNT. For the view that anarchism represents artisanal interests see Pierre Ansert, *Naissance de l'anarchisme* (Paris, 1970); for an interpretation emphasizing its appeal to landless rural workers see Hobsbawm, *Primitive Rebels* (New York, 1959), pp. 74–92; Aimé Berthod stresses the affinities between Proudhon's anarchism and peasant interests in *Proudhon et la propriété* (Paris, 1910); the association of anarchism with 'petty bourgeois' interests is, of course, a Marxist hobbyhorse.

23 John Chapman and Gerald Gaus decry this aspiration as self-contradictory in their provocative essay, 'Anarchism and Political Philosophy: An Introduction', in Pennock and Chapman (eds.), *Anarchism*, p. xi. They also cite Eric Voegelin for denouncing it as 'the pneumatic disease', p. xliii. In ch. 1 of his *Hegel* (Cambridge, England, 1975), Charles Taylor gives a magisterial account of our preoccupation with individuality and community in the context of the development of pre-Hegelian German philosophy and culture.

INDEX

Index

Gaus, Gerald, 184 n23
Gide, André, 47
Godwin, William: criticism of
government, 127; criticism of law,
156; not an elitist, 95–6; not a
utilitarian, 115; on authority, 67,
174 n9; on censure, 9, 13–14; on
community, 26–7, 29, 30, 40, 42,
77, 81; on conversation, 42–3, 47;
on democracy, 63–5; on
economics, 126; on equality,
76–9, 93; on freedom, 9, 11, 13,
28, 31; on individuality, 26, 28,
29, 30, 31, 41–2, 77, 81, 117, 141;
on justice, 77–9; on privacy, 48,
140, 141, 172 n29; on property,
78; his psychology, 119, 157; on
punishment, 72–6; on sincerity,
40, 43–9; on strategy, 90–7; on
technology, 83, 84–5
Gottlieb, Lou, 162
government: anarchist criticism of,
22–4, 36–9, 121–3, 127; compared
to censure, 18–23, 36–8; liberal
view of, 120–2; as means to
anarchy, 138
Guerin, Daniel, 109–10, 112

Hegel, G. W. F., 3–5, 166
Henry, Fortuné, 183 n15
Hocking, William E., 113, 114, 117,
123
Horowitz, Irving, 89
human nature, 118
Hyndman, Edward, 140

incrementalism, 154–5
individuality: anarchist conception
of, 26; and community, 29–31,
137–8, 139–40, 169 n15; and
freedom, 27–8; liberal versus
anarchist, 117; J. S. Mill's, 116

Jaszi, Oscar, 112
Jouvenel, Bertrand de, 180 n24
justice, distributive, 77–9, 81, 143–4

Kant, Immanuel, 114, 118, 121
Kateb, George, 178 n67
Kropotkin, Peter: not a utilitarian,
115–16; on anarchist society,
58–9, 81–2, 141, 175 n52; on
benevolence, 40, 56–9; on

censure, 9; on community, 26–7,
28, 30, 40, 57–8, 81, 173 n57; on
democracy, 106; on economics,
126; on equality, 76, 80–3; on the
family, 173 n57; on freedom, 9;
on individuality, 26, 30, 57, 81,
117; on property, 80; on
proto-anarchism, 139; his
psychology, 119–20; on respect,
56; on strategy, 105–9, 153; on
technology, 84–7

Landauer, Karl, 158
law, 18–23, 36–8, 155–6, 168 n22
liberals, 113–24
liberty, see freedom
Locke, John, 118

Mack, Mary P., 180 n26
Marx, Karl, 3–5, 102, 124–9, 135,
152, 166, 175 n56
Mazor, Lester, 156
Mill, John Stuart, 114, 117, 122–3,
140
Miller, David, 175 n47
Monro, D. H., 179 n9, 179 n22
Morningstar Ranch, 162

New Left, 164
Nietzsche, Friedrich, 46–7

Paine, Thomas, 120
Pannekoek, Anton, 130
Paterson, R. W. K., 167 n8
Paul, William, 130, 131
Plamenatz, John, 181 n34
Plato, 135
Plekhanov, George, 25
Priestley, J. B., 179 n9
privacy, 48, 140–1
Proby, William, 2, 24, 38
Proudhon, Pierre-Joseph: criticism
of government, 127; criticism of
utilitarianism, 116; on anarchist
society, 50–1; on authority, 69–70,
174 n9; on benevolence, 56; on
censure, 32; on community, 26–7,
28, 50; on education, 51–2; on
equality, 79; on the family, 52–3,
172 n45; on freedom, 9, 12, 28;
on individuality, 26, 28, 49–50; on
internalization, 14–16, 32; his
psychology, 118; on punishment,

186

Index

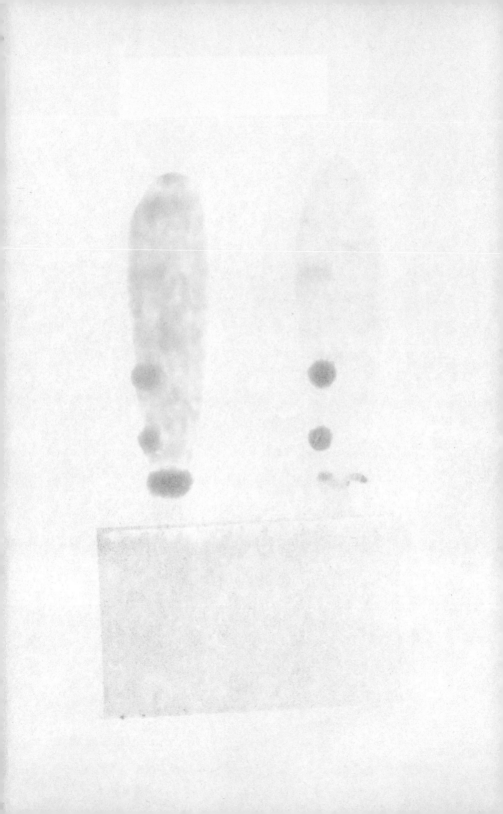